This bo
10659996

Leigh Michaels

is the author of more than 70 contemporary romance novels published by Harlequin Books. More than 30 million copies of her books have been printed worldwide. Her work has been translated and published in 120 countries in more than 20 languages, including Russian and Chinese. Six of her books have been finalists for Best Traditional Romance novel in the RITA contest sponsored by Romance Writers of America.

She is the author of **WRITING THE ROMANCE NOVEL, a** how-to guide, and has produced audio tapes on such subjects as conflict, writer's block, and the difficulty of creating realistic characters of the opposite sex.

She teaches romance writing at the University of Iowa and at www.writingclasses.com (Gotham Writers' Workshop). Men and women from around the world have participated in her workshops, and a number of them have gone on to publish their own romance novels with commercial publishers.

She has written magazine articles for *Writer's Digest* and *the Writer* and is a frequent contributor to *Romance Writers Report*, the professional journal of the Romance Writers of America.

She wrote her first romance novel when she was fifteen and burned it, then wrote and burned five more complete manuscripts in the next ten years before submitting to a publisher. Her first submission was accepted and published by Harlequin, the first publisher to look at it.

A native Iowan, she received her bachelor of arts degree in journalism from Drake University in Des Moines, Iowa, finishing her degree program in three years and graduating summa cum laude.

Creating Romantic Characters

Bringing Life to
Your Romance Novel

Leigh Michaels

PBL Limited
Ottumwa IA

Over The Author's Shoulder

I've written and studied writing all my life, and I can't begin to count the times when I've stopped dead in the middle of a story and said, "That's fantastic! I wonder what inspired the author to do it *that* way." What I would give, for instance, to sit down for half an hour (though a week would be better) and talk to J.R.R. Tolkien about exactly how he traveled from the random sentence "In a hole in the ground there lived a hobbit," which he scrawled on an exam paper he was grading, to the *Lord of the Rings* trilogy.

I say that because it feels pretty egotistical to be writing a how-to-write book using examples from my own work. I hope that when you finish reading this book, you'll be pleased to have had the opportunity to look over the author's shoulder, as it were, as we share the process of creating and showing characters.

*****

This book is dedicated to the memory of Jacqui Bianchi, editorial director of Mills & Boon and my first editor, who gently taught me much of what I know about characters.

My most sincere thanks go to my husband, who figuratively held my hand and literally kept my coffee cup filled while I wrote; to Andre Becker and Alex Steele of Gotham Writers' Workshop, who facilitated the process; to Elaine Orr, who provided a much needed distance and perspective; and to my students, who inspired this effort.

Thank you all. I hope you will enjoy the result.

Table of Contents

The World of Romance

The history of romance novels

Love and romance have always been just as much in demand in the literary world as in real life, but the romance novel as we know it today originated in the early twentieth century in England. The publishing firm of Mills & Boon, established in about 1910, brought out the work of such authors as Agatha Christie and Jack London– and also published romantic fiction..[1] Soon the firm realized that its hardcover romances, sold mostly to libraries, were in more demand than many of its regular titles were. As the years passed, romantic fiction outstripped other sales, and eventually the firm dropped most other types of books in order to concentrate on publishing romance novels.

In the 1950s the success of Mills & Boon romances was noted by a Canadian publisher, Harlequin Books. The two firms began to cooperate, with Harlequin publishing in North America many of the titles Mills & Boon was releasing in the United Kingdom. The two firms merged in the early 1970s, with Mills & Boon becoming a branch office of Harlequin (itself a division of the Torstar corporation). For a number of years Mills & Boon continued to be the acquiring editorial office, buying books mostly from British

---

[1] For a deeper discussion of the history of romance, consult jay (sic) Dixon's *The Romantic Fiction of Mills & Boon*, UCL Press, London, 1999.

authors. Though they published American author Janet Dailey, it wasn't until the early 1980s that the market truly opened to other Americans.

For many years there was only one brand of romance novel, known almost generically in the United Kingdom as a "Mills & Boon" and in North America as a "Harlequin." Despite the lack of brand-name variety, however, the stories were already widely divergent– contemporary, medical, and historical romances were all published under the same imprint.

But readers who gobbled up those original romances wanted even more variety, and authors wanted to stretch their wings with different kinds of stories–longer, spicier, more sensual, including elements that just didn't fit in the short, sweet, traditional package.

(When the boundaries began to expand, no one was quite certain about where they were going to end up. My first editor told me about sitting down to lunch at the Ritz Hotel in London with a well-established author. As the waiters set their appetizers in front of them, the middle-aged female author leaned over to the very young female editor and boomed, "Now tell me, dear, just how much sex can I have?")

Varieties of romance novels

In the 1970s, individual types of romances began to split off from the long-established core. Radically different cover designs and distinctive brand names made the various styles of stories more easily distinguished at the point of purchase.

At about the same time, other publishers picked up on the success of the Harlequin/Mills & Boon machine, and new lines, styles, and types of romance novels began to appear in the marketplace. Not long afterward, some of those lines began to disappear again, as publishers discovered that a successful romance novel required more than simply *handsome boy meets cute girl*. Since then the romance market has been an ever-changing kaleidoscope.

Some memorable (though now defunct) lines included Silhouette Shadows, which featured paranormal plots verging on soft-core horror; Lucky In Love, which required a main character to have suddenly struck it rich; and Second Chance at Love, which starred older heroes or heroines who had been widowed or divorced.

At any given time there are at least twenty "lines" or "series" or "categories" of romance novels. Category romances are books which have certain elements in common (for instance, they all involve a mystery as well as the romance, or they all are romantic comedy). Category books are packaged in similar covers and marketed as a group rather than individually, and they generally stay on the shelf for a month, sometimes less, before being replaced with the next group of titles.

In addition to the series romances, however, each month brings a bookcase full of new single-title romances– books which stand alone, are marketed individually, and stay on the bookstore rack longer than series titles.

Focus on love

The one thing all of those books have in common is that no matter what else is going on in the story, the main focus is on the hero and heroine and their growing love for each other.

Beyond that, almost anything goes. Romances come in as many types as there are kinds of readers. There are sensual romances and even-more-sensual romances. There are romances which include mystery, suspense, even espionage. There are romances which verge on mainstream in length and subject matter. There are romances which tackle difficult social issues. There are historical romances, both long and short, and inspirational (sometimes referred to as Christian) romances.[2] In all cases, however, the key is that the love story– not the mystery or the sexual details or the social issues– is the most important part of the book.

The definition of the romance novel

What is a romance novel, and what makes it different from other novels which include a romantic relationship? The distinction lies in which part of the story is emphasized. In a romance novel, the core story is the developing relationship between a man and a woman. The other events in the storyline, though very important, are secondary to the love story. In many other kinds of books which contain romantic elements, the romance is not the main story. In fact, in many cases the romantic interest could be removed without destroying the story. In the romance novel, that just isn't possible.

Is there a formula for the romance novel? Well– yes. And no. There's a basic structure common to all romances, but there's no step-by-step recipe to follow.

A romance novel is the story of a man and a woman who, as they confront and solve a problem, realize that the love they share is the sort that comes along only once in a lifetime, and then commit themselves to each other forever.

Man. Woman. Problem. Lifelong love. Happy ending.

---

[2] Romance sub-genres are listed and defined in the reference section.

That's the formula–the basic structure.

By that definition, of course, mysteries also have a formula. If you wrote a mystery in which a crime was never committed, or the suspected murder turned out on the last page to have been death by natural causes, or the investigator declared the problem unsolvable and went off on vacation instead of telling the reader what really happened, you'd soon hear about the importance of a basic structure.

Types of romantic stories

Within the broad range of romance novels, there are certain kinds of stories which crop up regularly. Some pay tribute to archetypal stories of the past, such as fairy tales. Others have come into existence more recently but have become traditions. Some books combine elements from several story types, while others belong to no particular classification.

The fact that two stories may belong to the same broad category does not make them alike. They simply have a common theme. Each of these story types has become a standard because it is a common fantasy among readers.

Here are ten of the most common story types:

1. Cinderella– Is there a woman anywhere who hasn't occasionally (even if fleetingly) wished that Prince Charming would come and whisk her off to a life of ease and privilege? In the Cinderella romance, the heroine is swept away from her normal circumstances into a glamorous world she had never imagined. But she isn't necessarily a kitchen drudge to start out, and she may initially see Prince Charming's help not as a rescue but as a complication to her already-difficult circumstances.

Cinderella stories are great fun because the sky is the

limit. That can also be their weak spot, because the more extravagant the surroundings are, the more difficult it can be to make the story logical and believable.

2. Beauty and the Beast– One character (generally the hero) is physically, mentally, or emotionally scarred, but the heroine is able to see past his flaws and deficiencies to fall in love with the sterling character underneath.

The more handicapped the character, the more difficult it is to create a fantasy happy ending for the couple. But though it's tempting to wipe out the handicap with a miraculous last-minute cure, it may be more satisfying for the reader to see the couple adjusting to reality rather than being rescued by a benevolent Fate.

3. Sleeping Beauty– The heroine is "awakened" to a realization of her worth, her beauty, her talents, and her sexual nature by her relationship with the hero. She may be young, inexperienced, and innocent, or she may be an older woman whose self-esteem has been damaged, perhaps by involvement with an abusive man.

The tough thing with Sleeping Beauty stories is to create a heroine who has legitimate reason to doubt her worth. The heroine who believes she's ugly even though everyone else finds her gorgeous is a cliché. Yet our heroine's wounds can't be so deep that it's hard to believe they can ever be healed.

4. Bad Boy– The hero has a tarnished reputation, sometimes for very good reason– but despite his past, he redeems himself and wins the love of the heroine. The frontier story of the schoolmarm and the outlaw fits this pattern. Occasionally the bad boy story features a bad girl instead, teaming her with an upstanding hero.

The challenge is to keep our bad boy from appearing to be a hardened criminal, an abuser, or a positively unredeemable soul.

5. Family Ties– Hero and heroine may have been raised together (perhaps as step-brother and step-sister), or they are related (perhaps as closely as second cousins). Incest taboos are at war with their physical attraction, creating tension in the story.

Family stories can go awry if the relationship is too close, which tends to create discomfort in the reader, or too distant for the incest taboo to be believable. Stories about step-siblings are more believable if the two of them weren't raised together from early childhood.

6. Friends Forever– Hero and heroine have a long-standing platonic friendship, or perhaps they're business partners who work together amicably but with no romantic involvement. When one of them realizes that he or she has fallen in love with the friend or partner, pressure builds on both.

The danger in stories about friends is that the characters often become so cozy and comfortable with each other that suspense goes down the drain.

7. Marriage of Convenience– The hero and heroine enter into a marriage not because they love– or are even necessarily attracted to– each other, but for reasons of business, money, protection of a child, reputation, etc. A variation is the engagement of convenience, where the couple has no real intention of marrying but finds it handy to have a fiancé hanging around.

This is probably the oldest of the archetypes, because the first telling of a marriage of convenience story actually predates the biblical account of Adam and Eve.

The difficulty of contemporary marriage of convenience stories lies in finding a sensible reason for two people who don't love each other to marry. Getting married simply to please an elderly relative or because the characters have been caught in a compromising position worked well in the romances of years gone by, but it's just too hard to belicve that today's young people would go to that length to placate a grandparent or to avoid embarrassment.

Authors of historical romances have it slightly easier, since past generations enforced different standards of behavior, but the reason must still convince today's reader.

8. Reunited Lovers– Two people who once had (and ended) a romantic relationship come together once more and try a second time to make their attraction work

The challenge is to create a problem which could believably separate the lovers and yet be solvable in the end. The interference of other characters (withholding letters, etc.) was a standard ploy in stories published in the past, but it isn't as convincing in books being written today.

Again, authors of historical novels have a little more leeway in choosing reasons for the couple's breakup, since society followed much different rules at various eras.

Reunited Lovers come in several varieties, some of which are story types all by themselves.

9. Secret Baby– The couple's earlier relationship resulted in a child being born, but because of their breakup the hero has never been told he's a father. In the current story, the heroine may admit the truth, or she may continue to try to cover it up. The hero may be delighted to find he's a father or hesitant to become involved. In either case he's likely to be angry over the deception.

It's possible to argue that *The Scarlet Letter* is a secret-baby story, though it hardly meets the definition of a romance in other ways.

The challenges of a secret baby story include explaining why the mother concealed the truth, why the father didn't suspect, and how the couple can overcome such a tremendous barrier and learn to trust.

10. Marriage Gone Awry– Though the couple's marriage ended with a divorce or separation in the past, they come together for another stab at making their relationship work. Sometimes they make the effort in order to provide a stable family for their child, or to prevent a custody dispute which would harm the child. Or they may come together again for reasons as diverse as a family funeral or a suspicion that there was something wrong with their divorce and they (surprise!) might still be married.

The obstacle to a believable marriage-gone-awry story is to create an obstacle large enough to believably end a marriage without making either party look petty or difficult, but not so large that it can't be solved in the end.

Teaser

1. Each story type listed here has many variations, and there are many story types not included in this list. How many more story types and variations can you think of?

2. Does one story type appeal to you more than others? If so, why?

Heroic Characters

No matter how exciting the action is, it's not the plot that we remember when we think back on the books we've enjoyed the most. It's the characters who stay in our hearts long after the book is stored on the shelf.

The plot is what happens during the book. The action sequences are how it happens. The conflict is why it happens. But it's the characters who make all those other elements– the plot, the action, and the conflict– both important and memorable.

A story can't hold the reader's attention for long if the events in it happen to a person whom the reader finds tedious or uninteresting.

The challenge for the author is to create characters that the reader will care about. Whether the character is a hero or a villain, we want our reader to be emotionally involved with him– enthusiastically pulling for the hero to win, but also cheering madly when the villain is vanquished.

In order for the reader to truly care about the character, the person we're creating has to be believable. That means the character must be both *realistic*, so the reader can relate to him on a personal level, and *sympathetic*, so we feel the time spent reading his story has been well invested.

Making a character realistic means creating an individual who is a mixture of good features and bad, of strengths and flaws. And making a character sympathetic means that no matter what he does– whether it's good or bad– the reader can understand why he did it. It's not necessary to approve of an action in order to empathize with it. But if the reader *can* empathize with the character's reasons, even if he doesn't agree with them, the reader will be much more emotionally involved with the characters and the story.

The main characters in romance novels should behave in heroic ways. That doesn't mean they jump out of helicopters to rescue fallen mountain climbers, though taking that leap would certainly be heroic. We're talking about heroic in the sense of being just a bit larger than life, just a little better than most real human beings.

Standards of heroic behavior vary by line and type of romance, of course. The characters in a mainstream romance can get by with a great many things that the ones in a sweet traditional wouldn't dream of doing.

Teaser

1. Think about a character in a book you've recently read. How was that character heroic, in the sense of being larger than life?

2. Was the character realistic? Sympathetic?

The Heroic Couple

Heroes and heroines are the kind of people we'd like to be, if only our tongues didn't get the better of us now and then. If only we didn't do stupid things or fall down in public or embarrass ourselves. If only we were considerate and tactful all–well, maybe most–of the time. If only we could think of the right thing to say at exactly the right moment instead of three days later.

Heroes and heroines are allowed their petty moments– particularly when they're dealing with each other– but in important matters they generally take the moral high ground.

Kind and gentle

Heroes and heroines are unfailingly kind to those who are less powerful then they are for instance, children, animals, and the elderly. They are gentle; even if Aunt Agnes incessantly talks about her health, they don't snap at her or treat her like a nuisance. Heroes and heroines don't kick the dog no matter how angry they are. And every last one of them has an honorary degree in how to get along with a kid while raising him to be a genius.

Heroes and heroines don't gossip, and they don't generally take delight in the troubles of others, even when it's the Other Woman and she deserves it.

Unless provoked, they aren't even rude–except to each other. Even then, they're not hateful or vicious.

Wisecracks and smart remarks are acceptable; cruel taunts are another thing entirely.

Heroes and heroines don't lie

But "the hero can be economical with the truth," to quote jay (sic) Dixon in *The Romance Fiction of Mills & Boon*, particularly if his motive is to protect the heroine.[3] To illustrate her point, she quotes the hero of my 1985 book, *Leaving Home:*

> "I told (the other man)... that your father didn't leave you a cent. Which is literally true. He didn't ask me if my father had done anything for you, so I didn't tell him."

The heroine can be equally careful with her level of frankness, sometimes telling the literal truth in a way that is misleading.

Partners and relationships

Heroes and heroines don't commit adultery. While they may have divorced, they do not enter into a new love relationship while there is still a legal or moral commitment to a previous partner.

This restriction is largely a matter of common sense. If a person has so little respect for a spouse that he or she has an affair– whether it's physical or emotional– with someone new, then it's difficult to believe that he or she would be any more faithful to the new love.

---

[3] Dixon, jay (sic). The Romance Fiction of Mills Boon, UCL Press, London. 1999. Page 53.

To a lesser degree, the same rule applies to other emotional commitments. A hero or heroine who is engaged is most likeable if, as soon as he or she recognizes the attraction to the new partner, the engagement is broken off.

Time to mourn

Whether the previous relationship was ended by a divorce, a broken engagement, a jilting, or a partner's death, the character does not enter a new relationship until there has been adequate time to heal. Rebound relationships often don't last in real life, and they're not convincing in fiction. The length of time needed to recover will of course depend on the nature of the relationship. It will take much longer to grieve the death of a partner in a solid marriage than it will to get over a steady date who suddenly decided he wanted to see other women.

Motives and opportunity

While heroes and heroines have almost certainly created some of their own problems, they have not done so out of stupidity or short-sightedness. The character's father may have lost all his money in a stock scam, but it isn't likely our hero or heroine was fool enough to make the same mistake.

If our main character has caused his or her own troubles, it's generally for a worthy purpose–perhaps even a noble cause. Conversely, if the reason is good enough, we can have our hero or heroine do nearly anything, even if that conduct would normally be considered indefensible. (Breaking and entering? Sure, if it means saving a child from freezing to death.)

Like and dislike

Heroes and heroines must have logical, believable reasons to oppose each other. Neither of them tries to keep the other from achieving a goal just to be unpleasant. They're in opposition because the result if one of them wins will be that the other loses something very important.

Growth and change

Heroes and heroines should grow and change during the course of the story. They are intelligent people facing serious problems. Meeting the challenges will force them to look at life differently and often change their long-standing attitudes.

Heroes and heroines can't be perfect, or they won't be believable. But even in their imperfections they must remain likeable, even admirable, in order to be worth the reader's time to share their story.

Teaser

1. Make a list of character traits or habits that draw you to a person, making you want to be his or her friend.

2. Make a list of character traits or habits that turn you off and make you not want to know a person better.

from
Backwards Honeymoon
(Harlequin Romance®, March 2002)

In this selection from *Backwards Honeymoon,* Kathryn
Campbell, having discovered that her would-be husband is
marrying her only for her money, runs away from her
wedding just a few minutes before the ceremony is to begin.
She literally falls over the hero in her efforts to escape from
her father's estate before anyone realizes that she's
disappeared.

Kathryn paused for a moment outside the back door, then
headed for cover behind the nearest large tree and started to work
her way across the garden trunk by trunk. Her plan was so simple it
could be summed up in two words: *Get away.* She didn't care where,
and she didn't care how.

Her heartbeat slowed a bit as she increased her distance from
the house, and with the first hurdle behind her, she turned her
attention to figuring out how to get off the estate. Jock Campbell's big
Georgian-style house didn't look a bit like a moated castle, but with its
high brick walls and iron gates it was nearly as impregnable.

And getting out wasn't much easier than getting in—especially
today, when the guards would be extra alert in order to secure all the
wedding gifts on the premises, to say nothing of protecting five
hundred guests who were all wearing their best jewelry. And in a very
few minutes, as soon as Jock discovered her abandoned wedding
gown, it would become even more difficult to circumvent the security
arrangements.

She was chewing on that, trying to figure out the weak spot in her father's defenses, when she popped out from behind a hedge into the narrow driveway beside the gardener's cottage and tripped over a pair of legs sticking out from under an old car.

A growl came from underneath, and a body, lying on a rolling board, slid into sight. "What the hell—"

Kathryn's gaze slid slowly from the man's dirt-splotched sneakers past a pair of jeans so worn that they were barely blue and across a grease-smeared t-shirt. She focused on a pair of broad shoulders, a tanned, rugged-looking face, a thatch of unruly dark hair, and a pair of deep brown eyes that snapped with aggravation.

"Can't you watch where you're walking?" he grumbled.

"Sorry. I was thinking."

"Oh, you're one of those people who can't walk and think at the same time." He sat up, and suddenly his gaze sharpened. "You're supposed to be getting married just about now."

Kathryn looked through him. "You must have mistaken me for someone else."

"Really? Then what's that bit of orange blossom doing stuck in your hair?"

Her fingers found the stray petals and plucked them loose, then began to seek out hairpins, destroying the formal hairstyle Antoine had worked so hard to produce.

"Katie Mae Campbell in the flesh," the man mused.

Kathryn bristled. "Nobody has called me that since I was six years old, and I do not plan to make an exception anytime soon. Miss Campbell will do. Or, if you insist, you can call me Miss Kathryn."

"And as I'm saying it, I should pull my forelock respectfully like a good peasant, I suppose." He rose slowly, with a panther's grace, and reached for a rag lying on the car's fender to wipe his hands.

He was taller than she'd thought; Kathryn found herself looking a long way up. "Who are you, anyway?"

"Jonah Clarke. My father is your gardener, in case you don't know."

"Of course I know his name. That explains why you recognized orange blossom from seeing a single petal."

"He'd be proud of me. Also he'd be charmed that you came to visit, only he's not here. He's over at the big house to attend your wedding. Which sort of brings us back to where we started."

It was none of his business, of course. "Why aren't you with him?" The question wasn't entirely a delaying tactic; Kathryn was honestly curious.

"I wasn't invited. I'm only here to visit him for the day." He tossed the rag aside. "So tell me, *Miss Kathryn*– what gives?"

"I'm not getting married."

"I gathered that much," he said dryly. "So what are you going to do instead?"

"I'm... leaving."

"I see. Well, if you're looking for your Porsche, I think the garage is still on the other side of the property."

She bit her lip and looked at him, debating. She was down to minutes, if even that long, before the alarm went up, and standing here talking was getting her nowhere at all.

"Jonah," she began. "You know perfectly well that I–"

"Mr. Clarke will do." He mimicked her tone. "Or, if you insist, you can call me... well, let's stick to Mr. Clarke. It's much tidier."

"Mr. Clarke," she said firmly. "You grew up here on the estate, am I right?"

He nodded. He looked wary, she thought.

"Then you must know if there's any way out of this place other than through the front gates."

He raised an eyebrow. "You don't even know me, but you're assuming that I was the sort who would go sneaking out over the walls at night."

"Well, didn't you?"

He grinned. "Of course I did."

"How?"

"Oh, no. I'm not telling you."

She caught at his sleeve. "Please," she said. "I'm desperate, here. I have to get outside these walls, right now. Will you help me?"

His eyes narrowed. "Tell me exactly what's in it for me—besides a whole lot of grief when your dad catches up with me—and I'll consider it."

She looked up at him and let her voice go sultry. "What do you want?"

"What are you offer—" He broke off and shrugged. "Oh, forget it. Katie Mae, you are too dangerous to be let loose on the world."

"I told you not to call me—" She paused. "Come to think of it, you can call me anything you want to if you'll just help me get over the wall."

"Will going through it be good enough?" He pushed open the side door of the garage and leaned into the dark interior. Then he dangled a large, old-fashioned key in front of her.

In a rush of gratitude, Kathryn said, "I'll give you anything you want."

"I'll think it over and let you know. Come on."

His loose-limbed stride ate up the ground; Kathryn had trouble keeping up with him as he plunged deeper into the woods which filled a good part of the Campbell estate.

"So where are you headed?" he asked over his shoulder.

"You don't think I'd tell you, surely."

"That probably means you don't know."

"No, it means I expect you'd turn around and sell the information to my father."

"Sure I will. I'll march right up to him and said, 'Jock, old buddy, I can tell you where your daughter went, and I know because she confided in me while I was hoisting her over the wall.' I'm sure he'd reward me, probably right after he slugged me in the face."

"What about the key? I thought that meant there was a door or something."

"You don't think I'd tell him all my secrets, do you? He'd have it sealed up in a minute, and who knows— I might want it again someday."

"Thinking of moving back in with your father, are you?" she asked sweetly.

"It wouldn't be my first choice, but you never know what might come up." He stopped abruptly. "Here."

Kathryn could see the vine-shrouded wall beyond the last row of trees, but she couldn't see anything that resembled a gate or a door. "Where?"

"Good disguise, isn't it?" he said cheerfully. "The vines were here when I found this place, but it took me a couple of years to train them just right so they'd hide the door without breaking when it was opened. Let's see if they still do." He pulled back a curtaining vine to reveal an arch-topped door built of heavy planks.

The key slid silently into place and the lock opened with a discreet click. On the other side of the thick wall hung another curtain of vines. Kathryn ducked underneath it and looked out across an expanse of pine woods that spread downhill as far as she could see, full of undergrowth and brambles. She looked uncertainly out across the dappled hillside. "Um... where am I?"

"Some Boy Scout you'd make. About five hundred yards through there is the state highway."

She bit her lip. "I suppose once I get there I could hitchhike."

"I'd suggest you hurry, or you'll probably be trying to thumb a ride with some of your own wedding guests."

She looked up at him through her lashes. "Maybe you should come with me."

He said something under his breath. She was rather glad she hadn't heard it clearly.

"Jonah... I mean, Mr. Clarke... you won't ever be able to collect whatever I owe you for helping me escape, if you don't know where I went."

The silence stretched out endlessly.

"One thing's certain," he muttered. "It's becoming obvious that I like pain. All right, I'm in for the adventure."

She smiled in triumph. "Then let's lock the gate and get going."

Jonah shook his head. "Not so fast. I may be a masochist, but I'm not an idiot. I was checked into the estate on the guards' list this morning. If I'm not checked out the same way, all hell will break loose and they'll be looking for both of us."

"Oh. I hadn't thought of that."

"Along with half a million other things you haven't considered, I'll bet. Anyway, I don't fancy being shot at by the FBI because they think I'm holding you hostage."

"Why would they think that?"

"Did anyone see you leaving?"

She shook her head.

"Did you tell anybody you were going?"

"Not exactly."

"Then they have no way of knowing if this stunt was your idea or someone else's. Look, we haven't got time to argue. You take off through the trees—just walk toward the sunset and you'll come out near a little roadside park. I'm going to go back in, get my car, and leave just as I normally would. I'll probably beat you to the park, but if I'm not there, hang around back in the trees till I show up." He pulled the vines back and stepped into the wall.

"Jonah," she said softly, and he turned. "Thank you."

"Don't thank me till we've gotten somewhere." A moment later the door closed with a creak and he was gone.

Teaser

1. What traits do Kathryn and Jonah exhibit which make them likeable? Admirable? Less than perfect?

2. What did you learn about the characters from their actions rather than their words?

3. Which character do you know more about? What kinds of things don't you know about the other character?

4. Consider the interactions between Kathryn and Jonah. How do they talk to each other? Treat each other?

5. Considering that they've just met for the first time, how do you think they feel about each other?

A Heroine to Befriend

Though there are always two main characters in the romance novel, in most books the major focus remains on the heroine, and the story is primarily her story. Though the hero's point of view and thoughts are usually included, the heroine's point of view and her thoughts usually comprise a larger portion of the book.

If the reader spends several hours reading the story, most of that time will be in the company of the heroine. So our heroine must be someone the reader can understand, like and respect– someone she wants to hang around with. Someone who seems like a real person.

That means the heroine should have a balance of good and bad characteristics, as all humans do. She should be pretty much like the people we run into every day at the office water cooler or at the supermarket.

Unsuccessful heroines

Many new romance writers create heroines who are perfect. They're not only shaped like Barbie dolls, but they never have to break a sweat at the gym to keep that perfect figure. They're smart and witty and run a multimillion-dollar business in their spare time. They've never cracked a fingernail and they can wear white shorts to a picnic and not get a single grass stain.

Or the new writer goes the other direction and creates a hapless, helpless heroine. This woman can't get herself across a room without help. She gets mixed up in one bad relationship after another, she'll believe any fool story she's told without ever stopping to consider the source, and she's wildly inconsistent in the ways she reacts to people and events. She's still gorgeous, but she doesn't believe for a moment that she's the least bit attractive. Because this woman doesn't respect herself, she commands no respect from others– including the reader.

Perfect Priscilla and Helpless Hannah

Neither Perfect Priscilla nor Helpless Hannah, in their real-life versions, are the sort of woman who makes a good friend. Priscilla, having never faced a problem she couldn't solve with the snap of her fingers, has no sympathy for someone facing real difficulty. (This is the woman who'll tell you exactly what you're doing wrong in raising your kids, even though she doesn't have any of her own.) Hannah is too busy bemoaning her own sad state to have time or energy for a friend–much less for doing something to improve her own situation. (It's such bad luck, she groans, that the last seven guys she dated were all users, abusers, or con artists...)

Women are unlikely to seek out either of these personality types to be a friend, and they're not apt to enjoy reading about them, either.

Disasters and crises

Readers quickly grow impatient with the heroine who stumbles into one disaster after another and has to be rescued. The heroine who has stupidly created her own problems– by making bad decisions or trusting and believing the wrong people– is much less able to command the reader's empathy than one whose troubles have come at least partly from outside. The heroine who walks into an obvious trap often doesn't win sympathy from the reader but inspires something closer to disgust. The heroine who believes a tale when it's perfectly apparent to the reader that the person telling it has a personal interest or an axe to grind is often not sympathetic but annoying.

The heroine with a past

A satisfying, sympathetic heroine is a woman with a past. That doesn't mean she necessarily has dark, deep secrets (though indeed she may have). It doesn't mean she's been a stripper or is on the lam because she's facing criminal charges.

Having a past simply means that our heroine, like all human beings, has been shaped by her experiences, and her reactions to what has happened to her make her a person distinct from every other individual on the planet.

Was she raised in an orphanage? Or did she grow up with a stern and critical father? Or was she the much-pampered only girl in a family of five boys? Those three women will have entirely different feelings about families.

The heroine's past experiences affect everything she does and every decision she makes. But it isn't necessary for the reader to know all of that history right away. In fact, one of the bigger mistakes made by most new romance writers is to pour all the information about the heroine's past into the first chapter. It's much better to wait until later in the book, when the reader must know about the heroine's past in order to understand her, to share that information.

Convincingly attractive

Physical attractiveness is one of the areas in which

romance heroines are a little different from real women. (When romance heroines are desperately unhappy, they always stop eating and lose weight. Now– honestly– how many real women do you know who do that?)

Though there have been stories and even romance lines which featured larger-sized heroines, these stories have generally been less successful than others in the marketplace. To some extent, this depends on the quality of the story. A wonderful story will be successful no matter what dress size the heroine wears, but a same-old, same-old tale won't sell off the shelves solely because the heroine is big as well as beautiful.

But readers' apathy about plus-sized heroines also reflects their desire for a heroine who respects herself. Our heroine does not need to look like a model or be shaped like one, but we like her better if she takes care of her body and looks just as good as she possibly can.

However, there is another aspect to attractiveness which goes well beyond good looks. The heroine must be convincingly attractive to the hero, and that's much more than having pretty hair, wide eyes, and a symmetrical body.

What is it about this woman that makes him want to spend the rest of his life with her? If she's a snot and a snip with nothing more than a gorgeous figure to make her attractive, our heroine is inadequate and dissatisfying, and the hero looks like a fool for not being able to see past the pretty face to the personality underneath.

The contemporary heroine

Today's heroine is independent, self-supporting, mature, and often career-oriented. She has problems– including some of her own making– but in general she's competent at running her own life. She may have had a bad relationship or even a bad marriage, but she's grown from the experience and our reader is confident that she's learned her lesson and won't repeat her mistake.

The heroine isn't desperate to find a man. She has interests enough to occupy her, even if she spends her entire life alone. She doesn't need a man in order to be happy or successful, and sometimes she thinks she doesn't even want one. She's definitely not going to settle for a man who treats her badly. She's able to adequately support herself both financially and emotionally, and she could keep right on doing so.

But when she finds the right guy, she realizes that the pretty-good life she's had can be a whole lot better if he's in it. He rounds out her emotional chemistry. Together, they're an unbeatable combination.

The historical heroine

The heroine of a novel set in a historical period shares many characteristics with her sister, the contemporary heroine– including a strong streak of independence and some feminist leanings.

This woman may have fewer choices because of society's restrictions, but she's determined to take advantage of every opportunity which is offered. She probably can't have a career, but she's not going to be sitting on a sofa for the rest of her life–she'll find work which is worthwhile to her and useful to others, even if her options are limited.

If she's had a bad marriage, it has ended with the death of her husband. Like her contemporary sister, she's willing to live independently for the rest of her life, though the realities of society may force her to consider a marriage of convenience.

The ideal heroine

My ideal heroine is a woman who could be my best friend. She has troubles but doesn't allow herself to be beaten down by them. She has a sense of humor. She listens, thinks deeply, and respects the opinions of others even though she doesn't always take their advice. She takes responsibility for herself. She's not necessarily beautiful, but she's attractive because she makes the most of her good features and she faces the world with a smile.

Teaser

1. What qualities does your ideal heroine possess?

2. What qualities would a heroine have which would make you want to be friends with her?

3. Do you think any careers are off-limits for a likeable and sympathetic heroine?

from
His Trophy Wife
(Harlequin Romance®, October 2001)

In this flashback selection from *His Trophy Wife*, Sloan
Montgomery has come to see Morganna Ashworth after the
death of her father. But Sloan has more than condolences on
his mind– and Morganna has some choices to make which
will affect not only her but her mother, who has been left in a
difficult position because of her husband's death.

It had been several days after Burke Ashworth's fatal car
accident before Morganna began to realize the perilous situation her
father had left them in. But as soon as she started to absorb the facts,
confirmation crept in from every side. The banker calling to demand
payment on the mortgage, the stock broker announcing with regret
that the value in Burke's portfolio was not adequate to cover his
margin calls—those things were only the beginning of a downhill slide
that seemed to have no bottom.

That was probably why, when Sloan Montgomery had shown
up at the house, Morganna had agreed to see him—even though she
barely knew him. Because, she thought, talking to him couldn't
possibly make things worse.

The memories of that day were carved into the very cells of
her brain. She'd been sitting with her mother in the drawing room,
receiving callers. A horrifying percentage of them had turned out to be
her father's creditors, and though she had tried to convince her
mother that there was no need to see each and every one, Abigail
insisted. Morganna could only watch with helpless anxiety as Abigail's

exhaustion reached crushing proportions. It wasn't until the stream of creditors had ended that Abigail finally agreed to go and rest.

Just then Selby had brought in a business card, neatly centered on a silver tray. Morganna could have screamed at him.

Abigail took the card, her hands trembling with fatigue. "This must be another one, because I don't recognize the name."

Morganna looked over her shoulder. "No, Mom. This one's for me."

Abigail checked the card again and looked suspiciously at her daughter. "You know this Sloan Montgomery? Then why haven't I heard of him?"

"Because there's never been any reason to mention him. Remember the fund-raiser for the women's shelter that I helped with last year? I met him then. He builds furniture in a factory down in the old commercial district on the lakefront—innovative, unusual stuff that he designs himself and he donated a bunch of it to the shelter. That's all I know about him." She looked up at Selby. "Show Mr. Montgomery into my miniatures room, please. Tell him I'll be with him in a moment, and close the door. Once he's out of the way, Mother can slip past without being seen and go up to her room."

Abigail had wearily agreed, and a few minutes later Morganna had let herself quietly into the miniatures room.

Across the room, Sloan Montgomery was standing by Morganna's work table, apparently studying a lyre-backed dining chair, smaller than his palm, that she'd been carving on the day her father died. "My furniture is a little different from yours, I'm sure," she said, and he straightened and turned to face her.

Against the background of tiny things, he looked even larger than life—impossibly tall and broad-shouldered in a dark gray pinstriped suit. He was every bit as handsome as he'd been at the fund-raiser, but today he was somber—more so, surely, than a condolence call on a casual acquaintance would require. The tension in his face made Morganna pause. She was worn out herself, or perhaps she would have thought twice before she asked, "Which category are you in?"

He frowned. "I beg your pardon?"

"I find myself wondering why you're here. I assumed this was a sympathy call—but perhaps it's just another attempt to collect an unpaid bill instead. Did my father owe you money too?"

"No, he didn't. And though I'm sorry about your loss, this isn't really a sympathy call either, Miss Ashworth."

Morganna frowned. "Then—if you're not intending to console me or regain what you're owed, why have you come?"

"To try to take your mind off things."

"Now that's refreshing," she said lightly. "And a great deal different from the rest of our visitors today. Half of them seemed to remember my father as a saint, while the rest were obviously biting their tongues to keep from saying what they thought of him. And those were just our friends— the creditors didn't bother to mince words. After all that, I could stand a little entertainment. Do you sing? Dance? Play the accordion?"

"I gather that you and your mother are in troubled circumstances."

"If that's what you call taking my mind off things— "

"Perhaps I should have said instead that I came to find out whether I can help you."

"I don't see how," Morganna said frankly. "*Troubled circumstances* is putting it lightly. Daddy's been dead just a week, and it's quite apparent that life as we have known it is over."

He nodded. "The house?"

"It's as good as gone—it was in his name, and it's mortgaged for more than it can possibly sell for. I suppose we could fight the bank and at least get a delay in the foreclosure, but to be honest, we can't even afford the utilities. Mother's already terminated the staff—though bless their hearts, they're staying on a few days despite being laid off, because they don't want to leave us here alone."

"There's no money at all?"

If she hadn't been so exhausted, so tired of going over it all in the squirrel-cage of her mind, Morganna might have been offended at the question. But it didn't occur to her to bristle at the personal nature of the inquiry. Perhaps from the outside the problem would look less thorny, more malleable—and she and Abigail needed all the insight they could collect.

"Nothing significant, compared to what he owed." She sighed. "Even if the insurance company pays off—and I can't blame them for not being eager to settle up— it won't be enough. I don't know what we'll do. Mother always left all the financial details to Daddy, but unfortunately ignorance is no defense. Just because she didn't know about his deals doesn't mean she isn't going to be held responsible for at least some of them. She's going to end up worse than penniless. And she's got no skills to support herself, much less to pay back debt—she's always been a stay-at-home wife. Besides, she's just close enough to retirement age to make finding a job very difficult, but too far away from it to get any benefits."

"But your father's debt comes to rest with her, right? It's not your problem."

Morganna bristled. "She's my mother. Of course it's my problem."

After a little pause, he asked, "So how are you planning to pay it all?"

"Well, that's another difficulty," she admitted. "It wasn't very practical of me to get a degree in art. It's hardly a field that's in great demand these days."

"You could teach."

Morganna shook her head. "Even if I had the temperament, I don't have the right education to get a teaching certificate— it would take another two years of classes at least before I could qualify. And then we're back to the problem of money, because I could probably earn enough to live on while I went to school, but not enough to cover tuition too."

"What are you going to do?"

"I start on Monday at the Tyler-Royale store downtown. A friend of mine is married to the store manager, and Jack— the manager— says I can arrange displays and try my hand at designing the storefront windows."

"That's a full-time job?"

"No, the rest of the time I'll be selling women's sportswear. It's a start."

She knew that despite her best efforts, she sounded tired and depressed. In a department store sales job, it would be decades before she could make a dent in her father's debts.

He said slowly, "I may have a better idea."

"I'm listening." Morganna shrugged. "Though I have to admit I not only don't see how you can help, I don't understand why you should want to, either. If you knew my father at all—"

It was apparent that he heard the question in her voice. "As a matter of fact, I never met him."

And then, while she was still trying to fathom why he seemed to feel responsible for her welfare and Abigail's, Sloan Montgomery had looked her in the eye and asked her to marry him.

Morganna didn't remember fainting. The next thing she knew, she was sitting on the floor, her shoulders cradled in Sloan's arms, her nose resting against the soft lapel of his suit jacket, breathing in the delicious aromas of wool and soap and aftershave. The moment she was aware, however, she began to struggle, trying to get to her feet.

"Just sit there for a bit," he said. "The last thing you need to do is fall down again." He supported her till she could sit up by herself, and then he perched on her work stool, looking down at her. "Apparently my suggestion came as a shock."

"That's putting it mildly." Morganna wriggled around to brace herself against the cabinet which supported the miniature house. "Whatever makes you think I'd be interested in marrying you?" She saw his jaw tighten and added hastily, "I didn't mean that the way it sounded. It's just that we hardly know each other. The idea of getting married—"

"I think we know enough. I know, for instance, that the Ashworth name opens every door in Lakemont society."

"Not for much longer," Morganna said wryly.

"That's true." His voice was cool. "Unless you act quickly to limit the damage from your father's peccadilloes, a hundred years' worth of family history will go down the drain and you'll be an outcast."

"Do you think I care about that? My real friends "

He didn't raise his voice, but his words cut easily across her protest. "And so will your mother."

Morganna bit her lip. It wasn't that her mother was shallow, she wanted to say. But it would be even harder for Abigail to start over than it would be for her daughter.

Morganna had already noticed how many people who should have come to offer their sympathies had stayed away instead. She didn't think that fact had occurred to Abigail yet, but she knew that when it did, the realization would be devastating. Even the poverty they faced would be easier for Abigail to deal with than the humiliation of losing the only way of life she'd ever known.

"Do you think I haven't tried to figure out a way?" she said wearily. "I can't simply conjure up enough money to bail us out."

"But I can."

She stared up at him. "Why would you want to?"

He looked across the room, over her head, and said calmly,

"I don't suppose you'll find this flattering."

He'd been dead right on that count, of course—for what he'd told her then hadn't been at all complimentary. He'd made it plain that it was not Morganna he was attracted to, but her social standing. With an Ashworth at his side, he'd be at the highest rank of Lakemont's society, and he would have achieved the final detail of the goal he'd set for himself as an impoverished kid years before—his own business, a few million in the bank, a position of respect in the community, a wife other men would envy him. Morganna was the ultimate piece in the puzzle he'd set himself to complete.

"So," she'd said, when the orange glow of her fury had finally dissipated enough that she could trust herself to speak without screaming at him, "it's not really a marriage you're proposing, it's a straight-out trade. Your money for my name."

"That's the deal."

"Usually, you know, it's older guys who have divorced their first wives who are looking for a trophy to display."

"Sorry to violate the rules, but I was too busy fifteen years ago to find someone unsuitable to marry, just so I could discard her now in order to acquire you. You don't appear to have any time to lose, Miss Ashworth. Are you interested or not?"

Morganna raised her chin and looked him straight in the eye. "Let me make this perfectly clear. For myself, I wouldn't consider this proposition for an instant. It's an insult and I'd live in a cardboard box and eat cat food for the rest of my life before I'd make a deal like that."

"But you have your mother to consider."

"Exactly. So convince me that what you're offering her is worth the price you're asking."

Teaser

1. What traits make the heroine attractive?

2. What attributes make her a heroic character?

3. How are Morganna's circumstances portrayed to make it possible for a reader to believe she would consider the hero's proposal?

4. Can you develop enough empathy with Morganna's mother to understand why Morganna would want to help her with her debts? Or is Morganna being a sap?

A Hero to Adore

In most romance novels, the hero is the second most important character– but he's also the pivot around which the story revolves. Because he's central to the entire story, it's very important that he be a fascinating character– one the reader wants to learn more about.

Falling in love

The hero must be someone the reader can picture herself loving. But we want her not just to *fall in love* with him, experiencing that dizzying, glorious rush of emotion– we want her to *stay in love* with him, and to believe that the heroine will truly be happy with him forever. Therefore our hero must have good qualities that will last through a lifetime.

Many a man is utterly fascinating to women but impossible to live with in the long term. The new romance writer often creates such a hero, and then wonders why the happy ending seems a little limp. A true hero needs to be exciting, sexy, and more than a little dangerous, but he also must have a solidity that assures our heroine that she can trust him and lean on him.

Today's hero

The hero of today's books, whether they're

contemporary stories or set in a historical period, has responded to the desires of modern women by becoming more verbal, more tender, and more vulnerable than the romantic hero of a decade or two ago. He probably doesn't feel any more emotion than men ever have, but he is more comfortable expressing what he feels. He is more likely to take a hands-on role in child-raising or in the chores of daily life. He can show his flaws, he can ask for emotional support, and he can display a sense of humor.

The strong and silent type still exists in the pages of the romance novel, but the reader is confident that under that tough exterior shell he's the sort of man she could love.

The wounded hero

It's possible, however, to make our hero so sensitive, so vulnerable, or so wounded by life that he turns into a wimp instead of a man. This happens most often when a female author, writing about the kind of man she thinks she'd love, gives him habits and characteristics that are more commonly found in women. This man asks lots of leading questions. He listens intently to the answers and invites further conversation. He pours out his feelings, often without even being asked to share them. He never fails to think— maybe even fret— about how his actions or words will affect the woman to whom they're directed.

In short, he acts more like a girlfriend than a hero. He's unconvincing as a man and vaguely dissatisfying as an object of affection.

It's also frighteningly easy to make our hero look like a fool. If, for instance, he's divorced from a perfectly terrible woman, the reader is going to wonder— with good reason— why he was stupid enough to marry her in the first place.

Alpha and beta

The alpha hero is powerful, driven, successful, and charming. The beta hero is playful and relaxed, but no less successful and no less charming. Both are equally welcome in today's romance fiction, though some lines are more suitable for one or the other. Each has his advantages and each can be a good hero.

Often the most attractive heroes display a combination of alpha and beta characteristics. A go-getter who's out to change the world between nine and five, he then comes home and plays with the kids, helps with homework, and tucks them in.

Now *that's* a hero.

The hero's reasons

The hero's actions, whatever they may be, must be backed up by appropriate motivation. He doesn't stand in the way of the heroine getting what she wants or needs just to be nasty. He always has a good reason why he must prevent her from succeeding in her quest.

His reasons must be explained somewhere in the story, though often the reader isn't allowed a good look at the causes of his behavior until near the end of the book.

However, even if the hero isn't talking about why he feels as he does, his motivation will affect all of his actions throughout the story.

A main character who interferes in the heroine's life without adequate and believable cause isn't behaving like a hero. He looks instead like a control freak or a potential stalker– possessive and perhaps even malicious.

A hero with a past

The hero's past experiences will affect everything he does. Though men are less likely than women to contemplate their experiences in an effort to extract a lesson, they're going to react to current situations based on what has happened to them in the past.

The fact that men are less prone than women to ponder their pasts can come in handy in the romance novel. A hero who is unwilling to commit himself to a relationship may not realize that his hesitation stems from his belief that his father was driven to suicide by a woman. He's more likely to think that every other man is just as reluctant as he is to settle down with one woman, and it may not be until he loses the woman of his dreams– the heroine– that he's willing to consider the causes of his feelings and change his attitudes.

Glitz, glamor and cash

The romance novel of past years often involved one partner– generally the hero– who was immensely wealthy and of the upper class of society. Fantasy is still very important in today's romances, and tycoons and self-made millionaires are as popular as ever. But across the entire range of romances, wealth is less prominent than it used to be. Though there's nothing particularly romantic about poverty, if the reader is convinced that the couple will not suffer from a lack of basic creature comforts, financial status is unimportant.

Far more significant than the character's income is his lifestyle–his level of satisfaction with his circumstances. Part of the fascination of a hero is his devotion to the work he does, whatever that work is. If he's a cop, he's dedicated to protecting the public–he's not on the force because it was the only job he could get. If he's a plumber, he's the best plumber around and probably owns his own company. If he's a tycoon, he's in business because he enjoys competition and innovation, not just to make money.

A character who is satisfied with a menial job is less appealing to the reader than one who wants to achieve in his field. If the hero isn't the boss, it's because he doesn't want to be, not because he couldn't achieve that level of success.

Convincingly attractive

The hero has to be convincingly attractive to both heroine and reader. What does the heroine see in him to make her fall in love and want to spend her life with this man? He has to be more than rich and good looking to be worth her time–he has to be good husband material, someone she can trust for a lifetime.

The historical hero

Of all characters in romance novels, the hero of a historical is probably the farthest removed from his real-life counterpart. Though there have always been men who regarded women as capable equals, they've been the exception, and society's rules have encouraged men to think of themselves as boss, head of the house, and final authority.

Sometimes the hero of a historical romance starts out acting chauvinistic, learning and changing through the heroine's influence as the story progresses, but even from the start he must have had a more open-minded attitude than most men of his era or he couldn't have made the transition.

The hero of a historical is willing to treat the lady he loves as a full partner rather than a chattel.

The ideal hero

My ideal hero is strong enough to be gentle. He's secure enough to let his loved one be independent. He doesn't feel threatened by the woman in his life. He's not so sure of himself that he believes he can never be wrong. He's a partner and a friend, not a dominator. And he has a sense of humor which allows him to laugh at himself and with–but never at–the heroine.

Teaser

1. What qualities does your ideal hero possess?

2. Are there any career choices or activities that you would find especially appealing in a hero?

*3. What's one thing you think even the most handsome, charming hero **can't** do if he's to win the heroine's heart?*

from
Dating Games
(Harlequin Romance®, November 1993)

In this excerpt from *Dating Games*, Rachel Todd meets her
hero for the second time when he rescues her from a
rainstorm– and possibly from a problem.

Rachel finished her hot chocolate, paid her bill, and made her
way to the door. The storm did not appear to be letting up; sheets of
water were hitting the front windows of the ice cream parlor, and in
the street outside ankle-deep streams were running. She stood with
one hand on the door, holding the almost useless umbrella, and
wondered if it was possible to get a cab at this hour.

She was so absorbed in watching the rain that she didn't even
see the man who was coming toward her until he said, "Excuse me."

Rachel jumped guiltily away from the door as if he had
demanded that she get out of his way.

Only then did he really seem to see her. "You're Miss Todd,
aren't you?" he said. It was the voice she had overheard from the
booth--the younger man, the one who was complaining about the
other one's wife.

Startled, she stared up at him. He had eyes the color of a
summer sky, wide-set and fringed with ridiculously long and curly dark
lashes. His almost-black hair was in need of cutting, and it looked
windblown...

The resemblance that had nagged at her earlier snapped into
place. "You're Ted Lehmann's pilot," she said. "You flew us to
Minneapolis last week."

It was not surprising, she thought, that she hadn't recognized him before. The cabin arrangement of the ten-passenger turboprop wouldn't have allowed her to admire the pilot's profile even if she had been so inclined. Besides, the conversation in the cabin had been far too absorbing to think of what might be going on anywhere else.

But she did remember the clipped tone of voice in which the pilot had issued safety instructions, and the way he had had to bend his head in the less-than-roomy cabin. She also remembered the butter-smooth takeoffs and landings.

He smiled a little. "Well, I'm not exactly Ted's private property." He paused. "Are you meeting someone?"

"No. It was so nice this morning that I left my car at home."

"And now you're waiting for the rain to stop? I hope you've got a sleeping bag." He zipped up his leather jacket. "Once it starts to rain around here it can go on for days."

"It's nice of you to be so encouraging, Mr.--"

"I'll give you a ride home if you like."

The other man turned away from the cash register and came toward the door, folding the top of an insulated paper bag. The two men had the same coloring, Rachel noticed, though this one was a few inches shorter. He nodded politely at Rachel as he buttoned his trench coat and then said to the man beside her, "I wouldn't worry about Camryn any more."

Rachel watched the young man's eyes light up. "You'll tell her to lay off?" he said.

The man smiled at Rachel. "Not quite," he said gently. "I'll tell her you're doing just fine on your own." The door swung shut behind him.

Rachel looked up at the man beside her, and was startled to see a reddish flush creeping into his cheeks. He needn't be embarrassed for my sake, she thought. Or was it that he was afraid she'd take his companion's comment as encouragement?

"Matchmaking friends?" she said crisply.

He sighed. "Family. Sisters-in-law, to be precise. I've got three of them and they're driving me crazy."

"I know the feeling." So that had been his brother. No wonder their coloring was so similar.

There was undoubted interest in his eyes. "You, too?"

Rachel nodded. "People think there's something weird about a woman who doesn't want to date. I'd love a ride home, if the offer's still open. Otherwise, I suppose this town has a taxi service, doesn't it?"

"Not much of one. You could be here for hours. Come on. My car's right across the street."

The vehicle he indicated was not quite old enough to be considered an antique, but it was close, and Rachel looked at it doubtfully. The interior, however, was meticulously clean, and the engine started with a throaty eagerness which reassured her somewhat. Besides, she thought, anybody who flew an airplane could surely keep a car running with one hand tied behind his back.

"It brings out the very worst in people, doesn't it?" he said as the car nosed out onto the rain-slicked street.

"Hmm?"

"Matchmaking."

"Oh, absolutely. Some of the combinations people suggest, and with a perfectly straight face—" She lapsed into a thoughtful silence. You know," she said, almost to herself, "somebody gave me a bit of advice just today about matchmakers. I wonder if she was right."

"What was that?"

"She told me that perhaps if I wasn't quite so militantly against the idea, people might mind their own business."

"And what does that mean?"

Rachel sighed. "That I should just go along with it, I suppose.

That's hardly any answer."

"You mean, you'd have to date in order to avoid dating? That makes no sense at all. Where are we going?"

"Straight down Waukegan Street, eight blocks. Say that again," she demanded.

"What?"

"About dating. You're right— if I was seeing anybody at all, the well-meaning busybodies would smile and stay out of it, wouldn't they?"

"Is that what I said?"

"And I wouldn't have to *really* be seeing anyone, as long as they all thought I was. That's what she meant, I'm sure of it."

"Don't you think the phantom lover would be a tough act to pull off?"

Rachel chewed on her bottom lip. "I suppose that's true. But if there was someone who understood . "

"You mean someone who's in the same boat, I suppose? My dear girl, if you're talking about me—"

Rachel blinked in surprise. "I wasn't, actually. But now that you mention it..."

"I could be all sorts of rotten things, you know. A rapist, a serial killer..." He darted a glance at her. "I could even be a political conservative, for all you know."

Rachel shook her head. "No. If you were anything so awful, your sisters-in-law wouldn't be trying to fix you up. It's that house there, the little one."

He pulled the car into the driveway and left the engine running while he looked at her thoughtfully. "Your logic contains holes that I could drive a truck through," he mused.

Embarrassment swept over her in a wave. How had she managed to make herself look like such a fruitcake?

She cleared her throat. "Absolutely. It's a silly idea. Forget it."

She tried to push the car door open. It was heavy, and finally, anxious to escape, she gave it a shove with her foot. "Thanks for the ride."

As she ran for the tiny front porch, she heard the rumble of the car engine stop. She looked back to see him open the door and get out.

Now what? What was she going to do if he followed her? He could be any of the rotten things he had listed, or a whole lot more...

But he simply stood there as the rain poured down, with one elbow propped on the top of the car, the other on the door. Then he called, "You've got a point. It's the weirdest scheme I've ever heard, but it just might work. All right, we're dating. Saturday night all right with you?"

Rachel swallowed hard. "Sure. Why not?" he managed. "Umm...excuse me. This is embarrassing, but— I can't remember your name."

Even in the rain she could see the sudden flash of his smile. "Let it be a challenge to you." And a moment later, he was gone.

Teaser

1. What traits make the hero attractive?

2. What attributes make him a heroic character?

3. How do hero and heroine interact? How do they talk to each other? Treat each other?

4. How do you think they feel about each other?

5. What do you know about each character by the end of the scene? What don't you know?

The Supporting Cast

Our main characters' story doesn't happen in a vacuum. With a few rare exceptions (like the occasional book where the hero and heroine crash-land on a deserted island), our main characters are surrounded by other people—families, friends, co-workers, authority figures, opponents and even enemies.

Secondary characters

These people are the secondary characters in the book. Though they're less important than hero and heroine, they act as a framework, a background, a contrast, and a sounding board for the main characters.

But the key word is *secondary*. It's tempting to let these side characters become too important in the book.

Dangers of secondary characters

There are fewer restrictions on the behavior of side characters. For instance, the heroine's best friend can be as catty and gossipy as you like, while the heroine needs to keep a civil tongue in her head— so sometimes it's more fun to write about the friend. As a result, the secondary characters can actually become more interesting than the hero and heroine.

It's also easier to write about what secondary characters are doing than it is to keep the hero and heroine face to face, whether they're discussing, arguing, disagreeing, or negotiating.

But the limited length of most romance novels means that there isn't much time or space for the development of these other characters. Even in the longer books– historicals and long contemporaries– where subplots and secondary characters are encouraged, it's important to keep the emphasis on the main romance. Therefore, secondary characters have to be drawn with broad strokes, and we don't include as many details about them as about our hero and heroine.

Tertiary characters

Third-level characters are the walk-ons, the extras who probably have no recurring part in the story. Because they're less important to the plot, they seldom have names at all, or they may have only a single name. The maitre d', the clerk at the store, Sharon the secretary... all fulfill functions at a critical moment in the story but are not important enough for the reader to get to know them better.

We really don't need to know that the maitre d's feet hurt, that the store clerk had a fight with her mother this morning, or that Sharon the secretary is worried about the child support check– not unless those details are important to the main story. Does it affect what's going on between hero and heroine? If not, then the detail probably isn't necessary, and it's more likely to be distracting and annoying than enlightening.

The appearance of lots of tertiary characters can be a tipoff to poor plot construction. Unless something important happens while the heroine is taking a cab to the airport– something that seriously impacts the rest of the story– then perhaps the cab driver isn't necessary at all. It might be better to reconstruct the scene instead, perhaps beginning at the moment when the heroine arrives at the gate to find that her flight's been cancelled rather by showing her chatting aimlessly to the cab driver.

Creating side characters

It's not a bad idea to take an inventory of your secondary and tertiary characters in order to see if they're all necessary. Can some of them be combined?

And before adding another character, think about your book as a movie script and ask yourself, "Is it worth the money it would cost to hire another actor to play this part? Or can I give the lines and the actions to someone who's already in the story?"

Teaser

1. Look through a couple of romances you've read recently. Besides hero and heroine, how many characters are there?

2. How much are you told about each character?

3. How does the author share this information?

The Good, The Bad, and the Ugly

Secondary characters come in all forms, from loving family members to enemies setting out to destroy everything and everyone the character cares about. Each of these characters can and should have a significant impact on one or both of the main characters, or influence the course of their story.

The significant third

A good many romances involve a very specific kind of secondary character, one who functions almost like a third main character. This person might be the child of the hero or the heroine, or it might be an adult who plays a particularly large role in the story. This character is sometimes the cause of the story, the pivot around which the entire storyline revolves, and therefore he falls into a gray area. He's not quite a main character, but he's a lot more important than a regular secondary one.

This character can create problems for the author, because of the need to keep him in his unique position at the edge of the main relationship–not taking over the main story. Many a romance novel has been destroyed by a significant third character who becomes too important.

The child

It's particularly easy to drift away from the main

characters when this important extra character is a child. We're almost programmed to put a child's needs first, and that carries through in odd ways when we're writing about a child. Furthermore, telling stories about what a cute kid says and does is often more fun than constructing a quarrel between hero and heroine.

It's even tempting sometimes to throw a kid into a story just for the heck of it, for comic relief rather than because the child is an important part of the plot.

Especially if the plot revolves around the child—for instance, the hero and heroine are the parents who are trying to settle the issue of where the child should live and with whom—it can be difficult to keep the story in proportion. No matter what the reason for the conflict between hero and heroine, they must remain the central focus of the story.

Send the kid out to play, or put him down for a nap, and stick to the main story.

Handling a child's conversation can be a challenge as well. Age-appropriate dialogue is hard to maintain, especially with young children, but baby talk gets tiresome (and hard to read) very quickly. Depending on the age of the child, use short sentences in standard English, or paraphrase, rather than trying to phonetically reproduce the child's language.

The parent/grandparent

Meddlesome parents, grandparents, and other assorted relatives used to be a staple of the romance novel. Now that people are more independent and less concerned about what others think of them, the managing relative is less useful to the romance novelist. But that doesn't mean the breed has died out.

However, instead of matchmaking or actively manipulating the hero and heroine, today's relative generally has a real problem or need, and the hero's or heroine's sense of responsibility means that he or she will be caught up in solving the problem.

A big temptation when dealing with a parent or grandparent is to let the story drift into details of the past, concentrating on things like the relationship between parent and child during the adolescent years– whether or not it has anything to do with the current story.

The extended family

Sometimes it seems that romance heroes and heroines come in just two varieties– those who have no family at all (or at least none that they want to speak to), and those who have enormous, close, warm-fuzzy families.

Family members can be terrific tools for giving information to the reader. They're likely to be delightfully and brutally frank, which can act as a catalyst for a main character's action or change of heart, and they know more about the hero's or heroine's past experiences than most friends do.

A danger is to get too involved in explaining the family relationships. If you find yourself detailing which birth order the siblings are in, or which brother was adopted and which was natural-born, or how their current quarrels and disagreements hark back to their childhood days, it's probably wise to think again and refocus on the hero and heroine.

The best friends

Next to family members, friends are the most likely people to speak their minds and the most able to influence a main character's actions.

Showing a hero or heroine interacting with a friend is one of the best ways to demonstrate what sort of person the main character is.

A danger is that friends aren't restricted, as heroes and heroines are, to speak gently or to restrain their actions. They can let it rip, and because they're talking to a friend, they often do. But if that tendency isn't kept under control by the author, the story can quickly slip out of control.

This is especially true with sequels, where characters who were previously at the heart of their own story reappear in someone else's. Sometimes sequel characters want to take over the new story, too. Beware of spending too much time bringing your reader up to date on recurring characters. The reader who missed that book wants to read *this* story, not be spoon-fed a condensation of the first one.

Male friends speak differently to one another than female friends do. Men tend to talk about things, women about feelings. Men tend to speak in shorter bursts and shorter sentences. Women ask more questions and are apt to pursue a subject even if it's clear their friend would rather not talk about it, while men are more apt to let it drop.

The villain

A truly powerful and effective villain must have something sympathetic about him, or he will be completely interchangeable with a dozen other forgettable bad guys.

A villain, whether in fiction or in real life, generally does not do criminal or cruel things just to be disagreeable. He generally has a reason– and to his mind it's a sensible, logical and excellent reason– for whatever he does.

It isn't necessary to present him in a favorable light, but if the reader understands why he's acting as he is– and perhaps even feels a tinge of empathy or respect for his reasons– he'll be a much scarier character.

Though it seems that the thoroughly nasty bad guy should be more terrifying than one who has a softer side, the reverse is actually true. The closer to normal the villain is, the more frightening it is when his twisted logic kicks in.

A villain who has no redeeming qualities is a caricature, not a character.

The other woman

The "other woman" in romance novels is a villain on a smaller scale. She's often painted as being a thoroughly disagreeable person, which can lead to difficulties with the story. If it's apparent to the reader that this woman is completely rotten, then how could our supposedly intelligent hero ever fall for her? And if she's clearly a self-centered liar, why does our supposedly intelligent heroine believe her?

On the other hand, if she has some redeeming characteristics and some logical reason for behaving as she does, the situation will be much more believable and interesting than if she's simply acting out of a desire to make the heroine miserable.

Teaser

1. In books you've read, how have the secondary characters interacted with the hero and heroine?

2. In what ways have the actions and words of secondary characters affected the actions and choices of the main characters?

Playing With Others

The heroine's friend, her boss, her landlady, the kid down the street–all can be important in showing the heroine's character, unfolding her story, and helping her to grow and change.

The key in writing about secondary characters is that we're using them to show an aspect of the main character. The focus stays on the main character as we show the relationship between the two.

For that reason, we give only the details about the secondary character which have an impact on the hero or heroine or on the main story. We don't go off on tangents about the secondary character's past experiences or relationships, his opinions, or her political views, unless sharing that information will enlighten the main character or influence his or her behavior.

Teaser

What kind of event from a secondary character's past could be used to influence a hero's or heroine's choices in the present?

from
Family Secrets
(Harlequin Romance®, August 1994)

In this selection from *Family Secrets,* heroine and hotel keeper Amanda Bailey copes with a hotel guest's child, four-year-old Nicholas Worthington– who's suffering just as much from being spoiled rotten as he is from chicken pox.

Nicky's fever was down, and he said his head felt better.

"That's good," Amanda said. "Let's pop you in the tub to soak while I fix your breakfast."

Nicky made a face. "Another bath? You'll wear me out!"

"It'll help stop the itch."

He considered, and finally agreed. He was splashing merrily when the bellman knocked on the door. He had brought an enormous suitcase on a luggage cart. "Mr. Worthington said you'd need these things."

"Nicky's clothes, I suppose? Not for a few days."

"It's mostly toys, I think."

"I don't need those, either--even if I had room for them." Amanda opened the suitcase to be sure. The array of toys which filled the case would have been enough to stock a small store. She shook her head in amazement as she picked out a couple of games and a few small toys, then snapped the lid shut. "Take the rest back upstairs. What I really need, John, is a single bed set up in the den. Can you do that for me this morning?"

"Mandy!" Nicky called from the bathroom.

"I'll be there in a minute, darling."

"Mandy, I'm hungry!"

The bellman gave her a sympathetic look as he lifted the suitcase back onto the cart. "Sure, I'll get the bed. I don't envy you your job, Miss Bailey. I wouldn't babysit with that little terror on a bet."

"Don't be too sure. Before it's over we may all be taking turns."

As she shut the door, Nicky appeared, dripping and dragging a towel. "I said I'm--"

"I heard you, Nicky. What a nice loud voice you have." She wrapped the towel around him. "But we have to get you completely dry first so you don't catch a cold."

"I don't want to be dry!" His voice rose to a steady wail. "I want a chocolate doughnut and I want it right now!"

Amanda sat back on her heels and began to applaud.

Nicky stopped in mid-shriek and stared at her.

"That's a dandy tantrum," she said. "I'm impressed. But I've got things to do this morning, so I'm afraid you'll have to put off the rest of the screaming for a while. As soon as you're dry, you may have oatmeal with fruit, or toast and peanut butter, or an egg for breakfast."

"I want a chocolate doughnut." His lower lip was thrust out, but he spoke quietly.

"If that's the only thing that will satisfy you, you're not so awfully hungry after all." Amanda reached for her blow-dryer.

By the time he was covered with lotion again and dressed in another of Amanda's tee-shirts, he'd decided that toast and peanut butter would be acceptable. He sat at the breakfast bar, with his chin hardly above the edge, and picked the crust off his toast.

Amanda watched from the corner of her eye as she loaded dirty glasses into the dishwasher. "Did your nanny honestly let you eat chocolate doughnuts for breakfast?"

He nodded. "With cocoa, too. I like cocoa." His voice was hopeful.

No wonder the child was impossible sometimes, she thought. With all that chocolate, and the sugar and caffeine it contained, he couldn't help but be over-active.

"Did you know my mommy died?" he asked soberly.

"Yes, Nicky."

"That's why I have nannies. Are you my new nanny?"

"No, dear."

"Oh. That's too bad. I like you."

Her heart gave an odd little twist. "I like you, too, Nicky."

Before she had a chance to feel sentimental, Nicky had bounced on. "Why do you have a bird inside the house?"

"Because he's a pet bird."

"Why's he in a cage?"

"So he doesn't get loose in the hotel and get hurt. If you're all finished with that toast, shall we feed a bit to Floyd?"

Nicky looked doubtful. "Will he bite?"

"Not if you hold very still and don't frighten him."

He didn't, of course; he squealed and dropped the scrap of toast before Floyd came within six inches of it. The bird tipped his head and remarked, "Strike one."

Nicky's eyes went wide. "He talked to me!"

Amanda, who was still astounded sometimes at how very appropriate Floyd's random remarks could be, tore off another bit of crust. "Do you want to try again?"

"Make him say Nicky!" the child commanded.

"I can't."

"Why not?"

"Because he has to think about each word, and practice. Can you say antidisestablishmentarianism?"

Nicky chuckled. "'Course not. It's too big!"

"All at once, yes. But I bet you could say it if you took a little bit of the word at a time and practiced long enough. If you keep saying your name to Floyd, he might learn it. But you'll have to be awfully patient, and talk to him every time you go by his cage. It might take days."

It took three more tries before Nicky could hold the bit of toast long enough for Floyd to snap it up, and another few minutes of coaxing before he learned to stroke the bird's pale blue breast feathers with the very tip of his finger. "He's soft," Nicky whispered, almost in awe.

Copyright 1994 by Leigh Michaels

Teaser

1. What techniques keep the focus in this selection on the heroine rather than on the child?

2. What does the interaction between the heroine and the child show the heroine's character?

3. What attributes of the heroine's make her a heroic character?

from
The Boss's Daughter
(Harlequin Romance®, August 2002)

In this selection from *The Boss's Daughter*, Amy Sherwood is caught in a dilemma—does she give her sick father the help he so clearly needs, or hold firm to her resolution not to let him use her any more?

Amy hesitated outside her father's hospital room. Then she took a deep breath and pushed the door open. No matter what Gavin Sherwood wanted to tell her, she knew that delaying wouldn't make it any easier to take, so she might just as well get it over with.

Inside the room, she paused to look at the man lying propped up in the hospital bed, surrounded by high-tech equipment. There was less machinery now than there had been three days ago, when she'd seen him in the intensive care unit right after his heart attack. He was still very ill, there was no denying that. But his color was better, and he was no longer nearly as fragile-looking as he had been a few days before. He was going to make it.

So whatever Gavin had on his mind, Amy told herself, she would listen patiently and politely and then do precisely as she pleased. She wouldn't exactly blow a raspberry at him, of course, no matter what he said—because he was still her father. But she wasn't going to be manipulated into making any deathbed promises to a man who clearly wasn't on his deathbed.

Gavin opened his eyes. "You finally got my message, I see."

He sounded a little querulous, Amy thought, and his voice hadn't yet regained all its power— or perhaps the feeble quaver was intentional.

Amy moved closer to the bedside. "Message? It sounded more like a summons to me."

"Took you long enough to get here. Where have you been? Out all night?"

As if he has any right to ask. "No, I got up early and went out for a walk. What is it you want, Gavin?"

"It's a bit involved, I'm afraid. Sit down, Amy."

"No, thanks. I didn't come for a leisurely chat, and I'd just as soon not be here when your fiancee gets back from the cafeteria or wherever she's gone."

"Honey went home for a while."

Amy lifted an eyebrow. *So she could rest, or so you could?* she wanted to ask.

"This has been an ordeal for her."

"She was obviously under a lot of stress the night you came into the hospital," Amy agreed. *In fact, she seemed to regard your illness as a great personal inconvenience.*

"She's very young," Gavin Sherwood said quietly. "She's never faced serious illness before in anybody she truly cares about."

And perhaps she still hasn't. Amy's tongue was getting sore from biting it, but she knew better than to say what she thought. Her father was already quite aware that his soon-to-be trophy wife was a major thorn in his daughter's side, so it was unnecessary—and hardly sporting—for Amy to take cheap shots at Honey's expense. Even more important, if she kept criticizing Honey, her opposition would only drive Gavin into defending his choice, further deepening the chasm between father and daughter.

But as long as Honey wouldn't be popping in at any moment, she might as well make herself comfortable, Amy decided, and pulled up a chair. "So what did you want to talk to me about? The message you left on my answering machine wasn't exactly chatty."

"The nurses were hanging around when I called. How's the job hunt coming along?"

"Quite well, thanks. Which I could have told you on the phone. So why was it so important that I drive over here?"

Gavin's fingers plucked at the sheet. "My doctor says I can be released from the hospital in a few days. But of course I'm still facing a long recovery. I won't be able to do much for myself at first."

"I'm sure Honey will make a terrific nurse," Amy said firmly. "It'll give her a preview of the real meaning of 'for better or for worse.' And she looks stunning in white."

"That's not what I'm concerned about. Of course she'll be there for me."

I hope you're right, Amy wanted to say.

"It's the auction house, you see. My doctor says I can't go back to work for several weeks, so someone will have to step in, and of course you're the obvious choice..." His voice trailed off as he looked up at her.

Amy was already shaking her head, and her voice was steady. "I don't work there any more, Gavin. Remember?"

"Officially you're still on a leave of absence, you know."

"I told you I quit, and I meant it. It was your choice not to accept my resignation."

Gavin didn't seem to hear her. "And if it hadn't been for that silly misunderstanding, you would still be there. So it's only sensible that you come back and—"

"*Silly misunderstanding?* I walked into your office and found you on the couch with Honey, and you call it a silly misunderstanding?"

"Of course you were upset, Amy."

"Darn right I was. Remember? That was the first clue I had that you were planning to divorce my mother."

"I know. And I truly wish you hadn't found out that way."

"That," Amy said tersely, "makes two of us."

"But to actually leave your job, to turn your back on the family business, over something like that.... Honestly, Amy, now that you've had a chance to cool off and think it over, don't you agree that you were being a little excessive?"

Amy considered. "Yes," she said finally. "I *was* a little excessive. I should have gone back to my desk and written you a polite resignation letter instead of screaming 'I quit!' at the top of my lungs in the middle of the executive suite while Honey was still trying to get her sweater back on. My technique left a lot to be desired, I admit—put it down to the shock of the situation. But if you're asking whether I have regrets over my decision—no, I don't. After a display of that sort of bad judgment, I'd have trouble trusting any boss."

Gavin looked at her shrewdly. "You can't expect me to believe that you don't miss the auction house."

He was right about that, Amy conceded. She couldn't honestly say that she didn't miss Sherwood Auctions. She'd worked in her father's business, in one capacity or another, ever since she could remember. Before she was a teenager, she'd been running errands, cleaning offices, watching the cloakroom. Later she'd moved up to writing catalog copy, spotting bids during auctions, and researching merchandise. And as soon as she had her degree she'd joined the full-time staff, though she'd still moved from department to department—taking a hand wherever she was needed.

Leaving a firm which had occupied so much of her life wouldn't have been easy under any circumstances, but that fact didn't mean she was sorry she'd done it. Once she was finally settled in a new job, she'd be contented again.

"It was time for a change, and I'm looking forward to new challenges." She knew she sounded evasive.

Gavin bored in. "Doing what?"

"I'm not absolutely certain yet. But just because I haven't

accepted a job doesn't mean I don't have any prospects."

"But the bottom line is that you're still out of work," Gavin mused. "Even after more than two months of looking."

"Blame yourself for that, because you paid me well enough that I could take my time and look around instead of jumping at the first possibility. And if you're speculating on why no one seems to want me— as a matter of fact, it looks as if I'm going to have three different offers any day now. Good offers, too. I'll have a hard time figuring out which one I want to take."

Gavin said slowly, "And each of them will give you a big change and a new challenge? Is that really what you want, Amy?"

"Yes, it is. I'm sorry, but—" She could afford to be gentle, now that he finally seemed to be hearing her.

"That's exactly why you should come back and run the auction house instead," Gavin pointed out brightly. "That'll be a big change and a new challenge, too, because you've always worked in the separate departments. You've never before tried being in charge of everything."

"And that's why I'm the wrong person for the job. You've got a personal assistant who already oversees all the details. Why not promote him?"

"His name isn't Sherwood."

"So maybe he'll change it if you ask him nicely."

Gavin looked at her narrowly. "You still haven't forgiven me for hiring Dylan instead of giving you the job, have you, Amy?"

"Where did you get that delusion? I didn't want to be a glorified secretary, making phone calls and excuses."

"Dylan is not a glorified secretary."

"Great. If he's been so involved in the business, he's capable of taking over for a while. I don't know why you wanted a personal assistant in the first place if you aren't going to use him to advantage."

"Dylan is very good," Gavin said, but Amy thought the tone of his voice sounded far less certain than the words. "But you know how personal the auction business is. It's a matter of trust, and I've worked for decades to build up that trust. My clients trust Sherwood Auctions because they trust me."

"So if you're saying that no one can take your place, Gavin, what's the point of asking me to try?"

"Because the next best thing to the Sherwood they're familiar with is a different Sherwood. It's just the same as when my father handed the business down to me, back when we were still selling farm machinery and odds and ends instead of antiques and fine art. His clients were willing to give me a try, because I was his son. And you don't only have the name, Amy, and the instincts— you've got twenty years of experience in the business."

"Only if you count when I was six years old and I handed out catalogs to bidders as they came into the auctions," Amy muttered. "I had to stand on a chair."

Gavin smiled. "And our auctions in those days were still small enough that a child could handle the weight of a stack of catalogs."

"Nostalgia is not going to change my mind, Gavin. Give your personal assistant a chance. If this hadn't happened, you'd have counted on him to keep the place running while you were on your honeymoon. What's so different about letting him take over now? It's just a little longer, that's all." Amy stood up and firmly changed the subject. "Speaking of honeymoons, is the date firm yet? Though I suppose it would be chancy to choose a day for the wedding before the divorce is final."

Gavin didn't seem to hear her. His hand went out to clutch at her sleeve. "All right. I didn't want to tell you this, Amy, but I suppose I don't have a choice."

Now what was he going to try? Hadn't he already run the gamut of persuasive techniques?

"You know, of course, about the financial settlement your mother and I have agreed to as part of the divorce."

"I know you made an agreement," Amy said slowly. "She didn't give me the details, and I didn't think it was any of my concern as long as Mother was satisfied."

"Well, that's the problem, you see. She may not be satisfied for much longer."

Amy sat down again. "Perhaps you'd better take this from the top, Gavin."

"We agreed to split our assets as equally as possible. After being married so many years, I felt it was the only arrangement that was fair to Carol."

"Also the only arrangement she'd have accepted, considering that you were the one who wanted out of the marriage," Amy said, almost under her breath.

"But it was impossible to split everything straight down the middle. For instance, Carol wanted the house and I—of course—wanted to keep the business. But because the values of those two things weren't anywhere near equal, I agreed to make her a lump sum payment as compensation for her share of Sherwood Auctions. It's quite a large amount, and it's due pretty soon."

"If you're threatening to withhold that payment unless I cooperate," Amy said, "you'd better think again."

"I'm not trying to blackmail you, Amy." Gavin fidgeted a little. "The fact is I can't pay Carol, because I don't have the money. My expenses these last few months have been heavier than I anticipated. All the attorneys' fees, you know.... I've ended up paying your mother's as well as my own, and the legal bills are still coming in. And of course it isn't cheap setting up a new apartment from scratch."

"To say nothing of the cost of tickets for a honeymoon in Italy," Amy agreed. *Poor Daddy— Honey's obviously been a lot more expensive than you anticipated.*

"It isn't as if I haven't been working on it," Gavin said. He sounded almost defensive. "There are a number of potential clients I've been working on for some time. You know the routine, Amy—it takes people time to decide to part with treasures they've collected. Time, and gentle handling, because they have to be comfortable with the decision. I was planning to see several of those people again in the next couple of weeks because I think they're ready to confirm some deals. But then this happened." He waved a hand at the machinery that surrounded him. "And I'm stuck."

"I don't suppose you'll be making any good-will calls for a while," Amy agreed.

"Without the personal approach, those people are likely to change their minds altogether, or else take their business to another auction house. I can't really blame them for thinking that they might not get the kind of attention at Sherwood that they would if I was there." He shot a sideways look at her. "Unless you take over, Amy. Because you're my heir, you see, the reputation of the firm is just as important to you as it is to me, so you'll work just as hard to uphold it."

"Or at least the clients will believe that," Amy murmured. "How could they possibly know the truth?— that Dylan is probably a lot more concerned about the reputation of the auction house than I am. It's his bread and butter, after all— not mine. Not any more."

"You already know, Amy, that perception is everything in this business. What the clients believe is important. And in any case, it's true—you've lived and breathed the auction business all your life, my dear, and whatever you say, you don't want to see it destroyed. All I'm asking is a few more weeks. And it's really more for your mother's sake than mine."

Cunning of him, to put it that way. Amy shrugged. "Now that's a thought. You could just turn the business over to Mother for a while. After all, she's lived and breathed it even longer than I have, and with her financial future at stake—"

Gavin's eyebrows tilted. "You're joking, surely."

"Well, yes, I suppose I am," Amy admitted. "But couldn't you just talk to her? Explain what's happened?"

Gavin shook his head. "I can't see her being very understanding. And I can't blame her, exactly—I got myself into this predicament."

He was no doubt right about his soon-to-be-ex-wife's lack of sympathy, Amy thought. Who could blame Carol Sherwood for still being furious over her ex-husband's behavior? Amy didn't think her mother would actually be short-sighted enough to put revenge ahead of her own financial interests. But she could understand why Gavin was hesitant to confess his predicament to Carol. If she did become vindictive, she'd be within her rights to demand her money even if it required Gavin to liquidate everything he owned. Amy could understand why he didn't want to take the slightest chance of having that happen.

"And postponing the payment for a few weeks wouldn't help much anyway," Gavin said heavily, "if the business I've cultivated so carefully goes somewhere else in the meantime."

Amy sighed. "All right. I'll see what I can do."

Gavin gripped her hand. "That's my girl," he said. "I knew I could count on you."

Teaser

1. What techniques keep the focus in this selection on the heroine rather than on her father?

2. How does the selection illustrate the heroine's character?

3. What characteristics does Amy display which make her a heroic character?

4. What techniques are used to show the two main characters to the reader?

5. What do you know about the characters by the end of the scene? What don't you know?

from
The Boss and the Baby
(Harlequin Romance®, May 1999)

In this selection from *The Boss and the Baby*, Molly
Matthews is a single parent trying to maintain her sanity as
she juggles her responsibilities to her daughter, her sister,
and her mother–while also trying to land a new job.

Molly Matthews straightened the lapels of her jacket and took
a deep breath as she looked herself over in the guest room mirror.
Her suit was stylishly cut, but the neutral beige wool didn't scream for
attention. The pale yellow blouse was softly feminine, but it was
neither lacy nor revealing. Her jewelry was limited to tiny gold earrings
and the slightly splashier pin nestled in the geometric pattern of the
scarf tucked casually around her throat. Her hair was swept back and
up into a neat twist, revealing a slim, straight neck...

And a bruise on the left side of her jaw line, halfway between
chin and ear.

Molly sighed. She'd done the best she could to camouflage
the yellowing stain with makeup, and she'd just have to hope that the
casual observer would think the shadow on her jaw was no more than
a reflection of the darkest color in the brilliant scarf.

She gave a final pat to the folds of the scarf and turned away
from the mirror. As job applicants went, she was as well-turned-out as
it was possible to be– tasteful instead of high-fashion, with nothing
about her clothes or manner which could create a bad first impression
with an interviewer. "Unless he's put off by someone who looks so
seriously vanilla," she told herself, and tried to laugh. But this

appointment was too important to make into a joke. The job she was seeking...

Though, to be technical, she wasn't interviewing for a job at all, she was vying for a contract. And she wasn't an applicant, exactly; she was a business proprietor contacting a prospective client who had indicated an interest in her skills.

If Warren Hudson liked her ideas and was impressed enough with her abilities to give her this assignment, she'd have a few months of work ahead of her. Enough, perhaps— if she was careful— to build a foundation under her new small business.

Matthews and Associates was, at the moment, very new and very small. Molly could see the whole of it, in fact, from where she stood. The bed in her parents' guest room had been pushed aside to leave room for a folding table, which held a telephone so newly installed that Molly hadn't yet memorized the number and a computer with the sales stickers still attached. Under the table was a box of office supplies in untouched wrappings, and a bag containing business cards on which the ink was barely dry.

She had bought carefully and frugally, but that corner of the room represented a good chunk of her worldly resources. Which was why it was so important for Molly Matthews and her fictional associates to impress Warren Hudson this afternoon.

That was the truly frightening part, Molly thought— being so very clearly on her own. Always before, even during a few weeks when she'd been between jobs, she'd had a safety net of sorts. But this time, instead of using her last paycheck as a cushion while she sought another corporate position, she'd invested it in her future. And— of course— Bailey's future, too.

Remember Bailey, she told herself. *You'd take a bigger risk than this for her sake.*

Molly picked up the dark brown calfskin portfolio that contained the best examples of her work, tucked it under her arm, and closed the guest room door behind her.

From the kitchen, Bailey called, "Mommy! Come and see!"

Molly paused in the arched doorway between kitchen and hall. For a moment her eyes rested on her daughter, kneeling on a kitchen chair so she was tall enough to work on the table top, industriously wielding a blue crayon. Bailey's dark brown hair, a couple of shades deeper than her mother's, was combed up into twin ponytails today, each adorned with a big pink bow that matched her corduroy overalls.

Bailey looked up at her mother and grinned, and Molly's heart turned over. *Yes,* she thought. *I'd take a much bigger risk than this for Bailey.*

"What a pretty picture, darling," she said.

From across the table came a light, almost brittle laugh. "Since no one could possibly guess what it's supposed to be, I'd say that's a safe comment."

Molly moved the crayon into a position where Bailey had better control and looked levelly across at her sister. "Hello, Megan. It's good to see you."

Her sister, she noted, had pushed her chair well back from the table. Molly wasn't surprised that Megan Matthews Bannister would maintain a safe distance between her creamy white cashmere sweater and Bailey's crayon. If Bailey had chosen paints this afternoon, Megan would probably have retreated all the way to the deck, despite the crisp breeze coming off Lake Superior.

Megan tossed her head. The golden highlights in her light-brown hair almost shimmered with the movement; though it was only April, the streaks in her hair and the tone of her skin made it seem as if she'd spent weeks in the sun.

But of course she had, Molly remembered. Their mother had written, in her dutiful once-a-month letter, about Megan's winter vacation in the Caribbean.

"I dropped by to ask Mom some last minute questions about

the anniversary party," Megan said. "I've been gone so much that everything's been on hold, but the details have to be wrapped up this week."

Of course you wouldn't be coming to visit me, Molly thought. *Even if we haven't seen each other in years. Even if you've never met your niece before. Even if we've been home only a few days...*

She was startled herself at the bitterness she felt—though the reaction was really nothing new. Even in their teenage years, Megan—popular, beautiful, and graceful— had never had much time to spare for a younger sister who had still been gangly and awkward, an unwelcome tag-along. And now that they were adults...

Megan's still the socialite, Molly reflected, almost wryly. Megan had married a wealthy man, from a good family. She belonged to all the best clubs, went to all the best parties, worked for all the best charities, vacationed in all the best spots, knew all the best people.

While I... Molly's gaze rested thoughtfully on the top of Bailey's head. The part which separated the child's ponytails was crooked and one of her bows had slipped, but when Molly tried to straighten it, Bailey squirmed away, more interested in her drawing than her appearance.

Molly gave up and looked around the kitchen. "Where is Mother, by the way? She said she'd watch Bailey this afternoon while I go to my appointment."

Bailey's lower lip crept out, and her chin trembled. "Don't want Gramma," she said. "I want you to stay, Mommy."

Molly's heart twisted. *Of course she doesn't want Gramma. The child hardly knows her. It's only been four days—*

She leaned over Bailey and dropped a kiss on her hair. "I know, darling, and I'd stay here with you if I could. But remember we talked about my new job? I have to go see a man— "

Megan drew a breath that sounded like a sharp hiss. "What

happened to your face? You look as if you've been in a brawl."

Molly's hand went automatically to the dark spot on her jaw. "Oh, this. It's nothing, really."

Her mother spoke from the doorway. "*Nothing?* She says Bailey kicked her." Alix Matthews's dark tone implied that she had her doubts about the explanation.

"Kicked— " Megan's tone was speculative.

Alix nodded and walked briskly across the kitchen. "In my day a child who did that— if, of course, she really did..."

"I told you it was a somersault that went wrong, Mother. Bailey didn't mean to hurt me, it was an accident."

Bailey frowned a little. She held up her drawing to look at it and then put her blue crayon down and selected a green one.

Megan didn't look convinced.

Alix's gaze skimmed over Molly. "That suit's all right, I suppose. At least it fits. You're not going to wear a ring?"

Molly wanted to groan. Instead, she said dryly, "Remember, Mother? I'm divorced."

"I still think that a discreet little gold band..."

Molly didn't want to listen to any more. "I don't expect to be gone for more than a couple of hours, Mom. Thanks for taking care of Bailey."

Alix didn't answer, but she looked at her watch.

Molly leaned over the little girl, and the scent of baby shampoo tickled her nose. Bailey was almost four, but she was small for her age, and her wiry little body still fit perfectly in her mother's arms. "I'll come back just as soon as I can, Bailey," she said. "You be good for Grandma, all right? And maybe tonight we'll go get ice cream."

Bailey's eyes lit. "Pink ice cream?"

"Bribing a child," Alix said, "is never a good idea."

Molly bit her tongue. The tip of it was beginning to feel sore, after four days of Alix's advice, but she absolutely would not argue with her mother about how to raise her child as long as she was living under the woman's roof. And if Molly pointed out the fact that she'd been doing quite well on her own, Alix would probably just sniff and say that opinions differed— so why bother to say it?

One more reason, Molly told herself, *that I have to do well in this presentation.* If Warren Hudson liked her work enough to give her a contract to produce his company's publications, then before long she and Bailey could move to a place of their own.

And that day couldn't come fast enough for Molly.

Copyright 1999 by Leigh Michaels

Teaser

1. What techniques keep the focus in this selection on the heroine rather than on her family?

2. What is your reaction to each member of the heroine's family?

3. What methods does the author use to influence how you feel about each individual?

4. How does the selection illustrate the heroine's character?

from
The Husband Project
(Harlequin Romance®, May 1998)

Kit, Susannah, and Alison are best friends as well as business partners, and when Alison has a problem, her friends are there with help and lots of advice.

Everywhere she looked, there were babies.

In the supermarket, they cooed and grabbed at bright-colored packages. In the park she passed each day on her walk to work, they toddled through tall grass and dug in the sand boxes. In the office of one of her clients, a set of twins napped cherubically on a blanket behind the enormous walnut desk...

Despite what she was seeing, however, Alison Novak knew that the Windy City hadn't actually had an abrupt population explosion. Human beings had a tendency to see what they looked for, and she was no exception. As soon as a person became acquainted with a new word, she was apt to see it everywhere from billboards to telephone books. Likewise, as soon as a woman realized how urgently she wanted a baby...

It was the first time she'd admitted that her longing for a child had gone beyond desire all the way to desperation, and the realization twisted Alison's heart into a pretzel. As if in answer, the pain which had for weeks been coming and going in her abdomen flared sharply. This one was worse than usual; it shot clear through to her back and brought tiny beads of perspiration to her upper lip.

Abruptly, she changed her mind about going back to the office and turned into Flanagan's instead. The small neighborhood bar was quiet and cool, and she could sit there for a few minutes till the pain calmed, as experience told her it would.

In any case, it was just half an hour till her partners would be joining her; the three owners of Tryad Public Relations met at Flanagan's every Friday evening for bratwurst and a wrap-up of the week's work. With any luck, by the time Kit and Susannah arrived, this attack would have passed and Alison would be back to normal.

She sank into a booth not far from the front door and asked the waitress for a glass of seltzer water with a slice of lemon. As Alison waited for the drink to arrive, she leaned her head against the tall back of the booth and closed her eyes, focussing her attention inward. Though the pain was a little worse than it had been before, it was following the same basic pattern--starting off like the worst stitch in her side she'd ever felt, and gradually diminishing as she sat still. This time it seemed to be concentrated on the left.

She was so intent on analyzing the discomfort that she didn't see the waitress bring her drink, and she didn't realize her partners had arrived till she heard Susannah's voice coming toward the booth. "It's perfectly awful, that's what it is.... Are you taking a nap, Ali?"

Alison opened her eyes and sat up a bit too suddenly; the dim little bar seemed to revolve for a moment, and Susannah's face, full of concern, swam before her eyes. "I'm fine. What's so awful, Sue?"

Susannah flung herself into the seat beside Alison. "The single most valuable piece of art the Dearborn Museum owns was vandalized this afternoon."

"The Evans Jackson painting?" Alison was startled. "How could anybody vandalize it?"

Across the table, Kit choked and started to laugh. "You sound almost like me, Ali. I wanted to know how anyone could tell it had been damaged. It was nothing but smears of red paint on a white canvas in the first place, so—"

"That was *not* what Ali asked," Susannah said firmly, and

turned to Alison. "Somebody sneaked a can of spray paint into the Museum and made a few additions."

"Maybe it'll actually increase the value," Kit murmured.

"You have no appreciation of modern art."

"Neither do you, so don't be a hypocrite, Sue."

Susannah looked stern for only a few more seconds before she burst into giggles. "That's true. And actually, I have to admit— only to you guys, of course— that it did look better. At least there's some variety now. However, when anything that's insured for half a million gets damaged, it's.... Why aren't we in our usual spot, Ali?"

"Fresh air." Alison waved a hand toward the propped-open door. "Fall's coming fast, so we'd better enjoy this while we can." *That wasn't bad for thinking quickly*, she told herself. She wasn't about to admit that ten minutes ago she hadn't felt like walking another step.

"It is warm in here," Kit agreed. "Though you look a bit pale, Ali. You didn't walk all the way back from downtown, did you?"

Alison shrugged. "It's rush hour. if I'd tried to get a cab I wouldn't be here yet."

Susannah slid to the far end of the bench seat, turning to stare at Alison with her eyes narrowed. "If it was the walk, she'd be flushed instead of pale, Kit."

Kit's eyebrows rose. "You're right. Then—"

Susannah picked up the glass of wine the waitress had set before her. "And it's not just today, either. Ali's been pale for a couple of weeks. I've always thought she looks sort of like an old-fashioned china doll, all shiny black hair and porcelain complexion—but there are limits."

"And one of my limits is when you talk about me as if I'm not here," Alison reminded. "Anyway, I'm fine. I'm just a little tired from a long week."

She didn't think she'd been terribly convincing, for Kit's eyebrows remained elevated and Susannah's blue-green eyes watchful. But to her relief neither of them pushed the question.

Kit drew circles on the table with the base of her soft-drink glass and said, "Sue and I have some great ideas for getting the singles club up and running, Ali."

Alison sighed. "Look, guys. I'm sorry, but you know very well I've been no more than lukewarm on the idea of the singles club since Sue first came up with it."

"You're the one who suggested getting a restaurant to sponsor it," Susannah pointed out. "And that's the key to—"

"One suggestion hardly makes me a fan. And I can't do a good job on a project I think is ludicrous."

"Oh, really?" Kit murmured. "What kind of public relations person are you, anyway? We're *always* doing something ludicrous. If you think I want to brag about creating a bunch of dancing ducks to promote the new water park--"

"But you believe in the water park," Alison reminded.

"Doesn't matter. Besides, you can't expect either Susannah or me to do it. You're the only one of us who can, Ali."

Alison sighed. "Because I'm the only one of us who's still single."

"Exactly," Kit murmured.

"That is completely illogical, you know. It's like saying I can't make a good video welcoming newcomers to Chicago unless I'm a newcomer, and that's just—" There was no warning this time, and the pain which racked her was by far the worst she'd ever experienced. Alison clutched at her abdomen. She'd have doubled up, but there wasn't room in the narrow booth.

Susannah's gaze met Kit's. "An ambulance, do you think?"

"No!" Alison struggled to sit upright. Almost automatically she said, "It'll pass."

"Sure of that, are you?" Kit sounded skeptical.

"It always has before."

"Oh, *that's* reassuring! How long have you been feeling this way, Ali?"

"Weeks," Susannah said darkly. "Remember, Kit? Clear back when you started having morning sickness, Alison was—"

If she hadn't been feeling so wretched, Alison would have burst into laughter at the sudden suspicion in Susannah's eyes. "I'm not pregnant," she managed. "It's just... cramps or something. A little worse than usual, but—"

"I'm relieved to hear it, Ali," Kit said crisply. "Excuse me for missing the occasion, but just when *did* you get your medical degree?" She didn't wait for an answer. "We're going to check this out right now. If you'll go get your car, Susannah..."

Susannah didn't move. "Are you sure I shouldn't call the paramedics?"

"I'm not sure of anything," Kit said. "But we can't ride with her in the ambulance, so we'll need the car anyway." She dug her cell phone from the depths of her handbag.

Susannah nodded and hurried toward the door.

"Oh, for heaven's..." Another wave of pain swamped Alison's voice.

Kit flipped madly through her address book. "I knew I should have put this number on auto-dial."

"I don't want an ambulance, Kit."

"I'm calling a friend."

Alison, taken aback, could only stare at her. *A friend?*

"A friend who also happens to be my obstetrician."

"I told you, I'm not—"

"—Pregnant, I know. Well, obviously there's something wrong, and the way you're clutching your tummy makes it a good bet that you'll end up consulting somebody in that field. Besides, Logan's the only doctor I can think of who's likely to still be in his office after six on a Friday night..." She turned her attention to the telephone. "Hello, is Dr. Kavanaugh in? I see. Will you page him and ask him to call Kit Webster? It's an emergency."

The worst of the wave had passed, and Alison could get her breath again. "I'm too busy for this. I've got a video to finish..." She was startled by the high, tight pitch of her voice and the panic which clutched her throat.

Kit put the phone down. "Exactly. And if you'd stop to think about it, Ali, you'd realize that I'm only doing this because I'm darned if I want to get stuck finishing your video." The words were tart, but her smile was warm and reassuring.

Alison's panic eased a little, but the lump in her throat suddenly felt as big as the Sears Tower. "Yeah, right," she said. "Kitty, I don't deserve you and Sue."

"Can we get that in writing?" Susannah said breathlessly. "I'm parked on the sidewalk, Kit, so it might be a good idea if we don't hang around here much longer."

Kit's phone rang and she turned away to answer it.

"I can walk," Alison said.

Susannah looked doubtful, but when Alison pushed herself to her feet, Susannah quickly offered her arm. Their progress was slow, hampered not only by Alison's discomfort but by Flanagan's other patrons, crowding around to offer advice.

They were almost to the car when Kit caught up. "Now that's luck," she said briskly. "Logan's at the nearest hospital, just finishing a delivery—so he'll meet us in the emergency room."

Alison sank into the back seat. There was no comfortable position; what she wanted to do was draw her knees up to her chest and howl. In a feeble effort to distract herself, she said, "Was his delivery a boy or a girl?"

"I didn't stop to chat," Kit said dryly. "For all I know it could have been a Federal Express package."

(*The Husband Project* is the third book of the
Finding Mr. Right trilogy. The other two titles are
The Billionaire Date and *The Playboy Assignment*.)

Teaser

1. How are the words and actions of the two friends different from those of the heroine?

2. What attributes make the three characters stand out as separate and distinct from one another?

3. What do you know about each character? What don't you know?

from
Husband on Demand
(Harlequin Romance®, April 2000)

A lack of communication causes Cassie and Jake to end up temporarily sharing a townhouse. Cassie's there because it's part of her job, as one third of an all-women service business called Rent-A-Wife, to supervise a contractor while her client is on a trip. Jake, in town on a consulting job, has borrowed the townhouse from his brother, the client's husband. Thinking he's surprising a burglar, Jake kicks in the front door, only to discover Cassie in residence. In this scene from near the end of the book, Caleb, the businessman Jake is advising, comes to visit as Jake is fixing the damage.

The magazine article made it look easy, implying that installing a new door was as simple as sliding a book off the shelf and replacing it with another title. In fact, Jake thought, it would have been easier to bulldoze the townhouse and start from the basement up.

He'd dislodged one rogue screw and was working on a second when Cassie came back with a plate lined with chocolate cookies. She hastily set the plate atop the sawhorse and waved her fingers in the air. "They're still very hot," she explained.

Jake reached for her wrist. "I was taught the best way to treat a burn was with cold water," he said. "And the next best way, if there's no cold water handy..." He put the tips of her fingers into his mouth.

Her entire body quivered, and she tried to pull away.

He shifted his grip and innocently ran the tip of his tongue along her fingers. The pulse point in her wrist was going crazy, he noted. Of course that was no surprise; his blood pressure had climbed to record heights, too.

Cassie said firmly, "You know perfectly well that I am not in need of first aid."

She sounded just a little breathless, Jake thought. Reluctantly, he took her fingers out of his mouth, but he didn't let go of her wrist. "All right," he explained cheerfully. "You said the cookies are too hot to eat, and since I spotted a smear of chocolate on your hand I thought you wouldn't mind if I just nibbled on you instead."

"That's the lamest excuse for a line that I've ever heard."

"I have others," Jake assured her.

"Don't I know it. Would you just knock off the effort to seduce me?"

"I promised not to push you," Jake pointed out. "I didn't promise not to remind you that I'm here— and to point out now and then that I'm still waiting for an answer."

"You've had your answer."

Jake thought that all of a sudden she didn't sound quite as sure of herself. "I'm waiting," he said gently, "for an answer I like."

Cassie gritted her teeth.

Now we're getting somewhere, Jake told himself. He lifted a hand to touch her hair, and the springy curls teased against his palm. He wriggled his fingers deeper into the mass.

Behind him, an amused voice said, "Knock, knock."

Cassie shifted her feet as if she wanted to run. Jake didn't move; he let the weight of his hand draw his fingertips down through the soft curls, and only when he'd finished enjoying the sensation did he turn his head. "Hello, Caleb. I didn't hear your motorcycle."

"No wonder," Caleb observed. "You appear to have other things on your mind. I came over to talk to you, but—"

"I'm going," Cassie said hastily.

"Don't hurry on my account," Caleb said. "I wouldn't be crass enough to make any further comments about Jake's state of mind. I was planning to say it looks like there might be some serious work going on here. In fact, it gives me a headache just looking at it, so—"

"Have a cookie," Cassie said from the hallway. "You'll feel better, and goodness knows Jake doesn't need any more sugar—he's jittery enough as it is."

Caleb selected a perfect confection and disposed of it in a single bite. "You're a lucky man," he said and looked longingly at the plate.

"Go ahead," Jake told him. "You heard me get my orders."

Caleb inspected the array of cookies and ate two more. "You know, Jake, if you're not careful with this Rent-A-Wife stuff, you may find yourself stuck with a long-term lease."

Jake grinned. "Because of a plate of cookies? Perhaps I should point out that I'm not the one who's gobbling them. If you'd like a regular delivery, I'm sure Rent-A-Wife would be happy to oblige."

Caleb didn't answer, but he continued to munch while he contemplated the idea.

Jake turned his attention once more to the recalcitrant screw. "I hope you don't mind if I work while we talk, but it's getting chillier and I think Cassie would like to have a working door before nightfall." He intercepted Caleb's thoughtful look and said, a little more sharply than he intended, "And no, that doesn't mean I'm henpecked. Lay off the whole matrimony question, all right?"

"I didn't even utter the word," Caleb pointed out. "In fact, I'd say it's an interesting problem as to why you have the matter on your mind."

"Because I've been thinking about your workers," Jake said. He was a little startled himself at how glib he sounded, for the retort was as inaccurate as it was prompt; he hadn't—consciously, at least—been thinking anything of the sort.

"I'm sure you can explain that to me."

Jake considered. Now that he'd started this, he'd better be figuring out what he really thought. "You want to keep your people.

Right?"

"It's a whole lot more efficient than hiring new ones and getting them used to my way of thinking."

"You're absolutely correct. But if that's what you want to do, it's time to start planning in terms of a maturing staff. As these guys get older they aren't going to be able to put in twenty-hour days and sleep under their desks anymore. They may not want to, actually—but even if they try, they'll be too stiff in the morning to work."

"If you're suggesting I put cots beside every desk and workbench..."

"I've heard crazier ideas. No, that's not what I'm suggesting, Caleb. But as time goes on your employees are going to acquire other interests—and other problems—besides Tanner and electronics. Things like families, and houses. If you can minimize the stress on them all the way around—"

"So I'll put your Rent-A-Wife to work full time, running errands and keeping everybody in cookies."

Jake glanced at the empty plate and said dryly, "Especially you, right? Actually, that's not a bad start, but I was thinking more in terms of things like gyms, weight rooms, on-staff counselors, activities that involve families..."

Caleb frowned, and said slowly, "That's going to take a lot of time to organize and administer."

"Time you won't be able to spend on problem solving," Jake agreed. "Have you thought about my suggestion? Hiring somebody to take on all the administrative details?"

"Yeah." Caleb sighed. "I have to admit that at first I was pretty burned at the idea of losing my job. Being kicked out of my own company."

Jake tried to conceal his irritation. "That's nothing like what I suggested. You'd be the same keystone you are now. More so, in fact, because projects would move along much faster if they don't have to wait for you to plow through the paperwork before you can look at them. That's what made your engineer quit—the slow process and lack of feedback."

"Really?" Caleb looked intrigued.

"Yeah. I got a hunch, so I called him yesterday and asked."

"Do you think he'd come back?"

"In a minute—if you were as accessible as you used to be. But that means bringing in somebody to handle the details you hate."

"Somebody like you," Caleb said. "Want the job?"

The capitulation came so abruptly that it took a minute for Jake to hear the rest of Caleb's offer. His jaw dropped. "Me?"

"Why not?" Caleb's tone was careless. "It's your idea. You could probably dictate the job description off the top of your head. And you've already got a grasp of all the important details about Tanner."

"I don't know," Jake said slowly. "I've never considered making a change."

And what Caleb was proposing wasn't just a change, it would be a major upheaval in his life. For one thing, it would mean staying in Denver permanently... and concentrating on one firm instead of flitting from company to company... and not spending half his time studying the next field, the next product, the next business...

Was the chill which crept down his spine like a slow-melting ice cube one of dread or anticipation? Jake supposed only time would sort that out. Time, and serious consideration—for he held far too much respect for Caleb either to jump on the idea or to dismiss it out of hand.

"Well, you think it over and let me know." Caleb reached for a screwdriver. "Now, let's get to work on this door so you can keep Cassie happy."

Creating Romantic Characters

(*Husband on Demand* is the first book of the
Hiring Ms. Right trilogy. The other two titles are
Bride on Loan and *Wife on Approval*.)

Teaser

1. How are the words and actions of the friend different from those of the hero?

2. In what ways is this conversation between two men different from the segment from The Husband Project, featuring three women friends?

3. What techniques keep the focus on the hero rather than on his friend?

from
On September Hill
(Harlequin Romance®, December 1985)

In this selection from *On September Hill*, Carey discovers that her sister's fiancé is not what he had appeared– when he kidnaps her and demands a ransom from her tycoon husband, Brandon Scott.

David was pointing the muzzle of the snub-nosed little handgun straight at her face, and he wore an unpleasant smile.

"Now let's go inside quietly, shall we?" he said. "Not that screaming would do you any good. There's nobody to hear you. But it would be a shame if I had to ruin that lovely face, wouldn't it?"

Carey said, "What do you think you're doing?"

"Making my fortune. Slide across the seat, now and get out by my door."

Carey obeyed. David's gun might be a small one, but she didn't see how he could miss at that range.

She got out of the car and climbed the steps to the cabin. David reached over her shoulder to push the door open. The inside of the cabin was dark, and there was a musty smell about it.

"Sit down while I light a fire," David ordered.

Carey didn't see any other option, so she sat down on a straight wooden chair. It at least looked cleaner than the upholstered couch. This must be where David spent his fishing vacations. Fishing for what, she wondered.

He put a match to an already-laid fire, then came to pull up another chair opposite her. "Now let's have a little brother-sister chat," he suggested.

"We could have done that on the phone." That she could speak at all was probably a minor miracle, she decided. Maybe it was true—when faced with an emergency, people could perform beyond their ordinary capabilities.

"Lynne and I have been doing a lot of talking lately, and we decided that it wasn't proper for Brandon to have your sister and brother-in-law on his payroll."

"I don't imagine Lynne will be turning down the trust fund he's going to offer her," Carey said tartly.

"That's a little different," he said.

"And Brandon's stepfather works for him, so I don't think you will convince him that it's improper."

"All right, smarty, you'll pay for that. The price just went up."

"Price?"

"We'd have been content for you to turn over the settlement Scott made on you. My information says it's a good size. But I hear it's tied up in trust. I also hear that if anything happens to you, it goes back to him."

"You're right." Obviously he knew all the details. Carey searched her memory. She didn't think she had even mentioned the trust fund to Lynne. She certainly hadn't confided the details about how the plan was set up; she hadn't considered that to be anyone else's business. So how did David know?

"If it isn't too nosy of me, just how did you get all of this information?" she asked.

David grinned. "It's perfectly easy. You're quite charming, Carey, but with as many people as you have working at your little brick dream-cottage, someone is always unhappy, or jealous, and ready to talk to anyone who wants to listen. Of course when my little friend let her greed get the better of her, and was foolish enough to get caught, it slowed me down."

"The maid I fired," Carey mused.

He nodded. "She really messed up my plans. So Lynne and I considered the life insurance idea, but you look plenty healthy to me, and insurance companies usually investigate accidents, especially if they happen soon after the policy is issued."

Carey didn't answer. She swallowed hard, remembering the way Lynne had brought up the subject of life insurance. It hadn't quite rung true, then, she thought; it wasn't Lynne's style to be thinking about the future. But Carey had been too trusting to be suspicious.

"To tell the truth, we'd almost given up on getting anything from you. But then dear Brandon gave Lynne her marching orders, and we just couldn't sit still for that. So we decided to take the quickest way." He pulled a small tape recorder and a folded slip of paper from his pocket. "You just read this into the tape-recorder, and I'll go call Brandon dear, and if he pays up, I'll tell him where you are. If not, well..."

"I wouldn't bet on him doing it," Carey said steadily. "I'm not exactly in Brandon's good graces today." She wondered what made David think he could get away with this. Perhaps he had no intention of telling anyone where she was. After all, she could certainly identify her kidnapper.

He seemed to have read her mind. "I don't think you'd like to see your precious little sister spend the rest of her life in prison." he reminded gently. "And if you bring me down, I'll drag her with me. She's in this up to her little chin."

Carey didn't doubt that he would implicate Lynne, but she wondered if he really thought that her blind love for her sister would keep her silent.

"Let's not delay, now," he said. "Put on your saddest voice, Carey."

Carey read the statement, but David decided she didn't sound scared enough, so he made her do it over. The second time her knees were trembling in earnest, and the voice on the tape quavered.

David played the message back and grinned. "That should wring his hard little heart, " he said. "Now if you'll just put your hands back here behind the chair..."

Carey, dazed, complied. "I'll take the ring," he said, pulling the diamond and sapphire engagement ring from her finger. "You can keep the wedding band. I never was too crazy about those."

She felt as if she were in a nightmare. This kind of thing didn't happen. But the jerk of her wrists as David tied them together and then to the chair told her that it was all too real, and she started to cry.

"I'd suggest you not do that, sweetheart," he said silkily. "Tears don't move me, and there's going to be nobody here to help you blow your nose."

He tied her ankles to the chair legs. "Lynne should have suggested that you wear jeans and a sweater," he added. "Not very thoughtful of her, was it?" It may get a little cold up here before the rescue party arrives. But I'll build up the fire and you'll be all right." He put another log on the fire and said, "Bye, sis. See you around."

Teaser

1. What techniques are used to influence how you feel about the villain?

2. What techniques are used to develop reader empathy for the heroine?

3. How does the selection illustrate the heroine's character?

from
The Bridal Swap
(Harlequin Romance®, January 2001)

When beauty queen Anabel Randall's engagement to Jax Montgomery comes to a shrieking end, her bridal consultant, heroine Kara Schuyler, is caught in the crossfire.

Kara left her car in a distant corner of the Century Club's parking lot and walked across to the main entrance. The day was gorgeous, even for mid-May; the breeze was soft and warm against her face, and the scent of lilacs drifted from the thick hedge which separated the first tee of the golf course from the wide lawn of the elegant old mansion which served as a clubhouse.

The elderly doorman, his uniform spotless and his bearing as straight as ever, greeted her with a smile. "We still have valet service, Miss Kara, and the boys would be happy to park your car."

"It's too beautiful to be inside any more than necessary. And since I'm early—" She caught a warning in his eyes. "What's wrong, Curtis?"

"Miss Randall arrived a few minutes ago."

Startled, Kara eyed her wrist watch. Either it was running slow and therefore she had an apology to make, or the unthinkable had happened and Anabel Randall was actually early for an appointment.

For once Kara ignored the delicate curve of the branching staircase which soared upward from the elegant foyer to the most private retreats the clubhouse offered, focusing her gaze instead on the enormous grandfather clock which stood off to one side. Relieved to see that she was exactly on time, she turned toward the double doors which led to the main dining room. The maitre d' wasn't at his post, but he'd no doubt be back any moment, and he'd know whether Anabel was already seated in the dining room or was waiting for her in the lounge which overlooked the formal gardens and swimming pool at the back of the clubhouse.

A door slammed upstairs, and the sudden crash drew Kara's attention—and her eyebrows—upward. A member having a tantrum? Surely not; that sort of thing was frowned on at the Century Club. It must have been just a stray breeze.

But the bang of the door had scarcely faded before firm, hasty footsteps sounded on the upper landing, and a statuesque brunette appeared at the top of the stairs. Kara bit back a smile. After a few months of working with Anabel Randall, she knew the routine well. The beauty queen always paused at the top of a flight of steps just long enough to draw all eyes, then she floated down with her head high and her back straight, seeming to barely touch each step as she descended.

This time, however, to Kara's surprise, Anabel obviously wasn't interested in making an entrance. She didn't even look around to check out her audience, just hurried down the long flight and brushed past Kara on her way to the front door. Her chin was high, her face was hard, and her eyes glittered. She was still gorgeous—but she looked ten years older than the last time Kara had seen her.

Kara called her name twice before Anabel paused. She hesitated for a fraction of a second, then slowly turned. "Oh, it's you. I forgot you were going to be here."

That didn't bode well, Kara thought. For Anabel to be early for an appointment and then forget it entirely— and not just a casual get-together, but a standing weekly date concerning her wedding, the most important event in her life this year...

"What is it?" Kara asked. "Is someone ill? Injured? Can I help?"

Anabel laughed harshly. "Jax should be grateful he isn't injured." She tossed a smoldering look up the stairs. "After what he just did... As for you helping, I suppose we might as well get this cleared up right now. But not right here. The last thing I want is to see that... jerk... again."

Kara's mouth went dry. *That jerk?* Anabel meant Jax Montgomery, of course. The gazillionaire fiance. The man who was— or at least had been—the love of Anabel's life.

Obviously he was upstairs right now. And just as obviously whatever had happened between them up there had been a disaster of herculean proportions.

Kara tried to fit the pieces together. Anabel had arrived early for her lunch date, something no one who knew her would have anticipated. And she had found her fiance... doing what?

This can't be happening, Kara thought. She followed Anabel out onto the veranda.

Without a word Anabel thrust a set of car keys at Curtis. Then she turned her back on the doorman and took a deep breath. "The wedding's off."

Even though she'd known that announcement had to be coming, Kara hadn't braced herself well enough; the words hit like sledge hammers. "But why?"

Anabel's gaze was icy. "Surely you don't believe that *why* is any of your business?"

Kara cursed her delinquent tongue. She knew better than to ask; of course she did. She was only Anabel's employee, after all— not her friend.

However, Anabel's refusal to answer was in itself an interesting response. While she wasn't the sort to get chatty with the hired help, Anabel had confided a few intimate details along the way— enough that Kara knew it wasn't purely principle which was keeping her silent.

So what had Jax Montgomery done which was not only bad enough for Anabel to call off the engagement but so wounding that she wouldn't even hint at the cause?

"It's off," Anabel snapped. "That's all you need to know." She strode down the front steps. "How long does it take to get a car around here, anyway?" she barked at Curtis.

Kara followed her. "But you can't just cancel a wedding." She winced at the sound of her own naive words. "I mean, of course you can, but it's not like calling off a tennis date. There's a tremendous amount of work involved in bringing everything to a halt—"

"That's your job. You get to be a wedding *un*-planner for a change."

"And are you even certain you want to? Just because the two of you have had a spat—"

Anabel turned on her, and the blaze in her eyes threatened to char Kara's skin.

Kara dismissed the possibility that Anabel was keeping silent out of remaining loyalty to her fiance, and she raised her estimate of Jax Montgomery's misbehavior by a factor of three. Had Anabel caught him with a harem, for heaven's sake? Deliberately she softened her voice. "I just meant this is a pretty big decision, Anabel. It can't hurt to give it a little time, to be sure it's what you want to do—"

Anabel's words were crisply spaced. "The wedding is off. Cancel it. And I don't want to hear another word about the entire subject, ever." Her convertible drew up in front of the steps and the valet leaped out as if he'd been sitting in a bonfire. Anabel slid behind the wheel.

Kara put her hand on the door before Anabel could close it. "Just a minute. It's not that simple. I can't just make one phone call and—"

"Why should I care how many phone calls it takes? That's your job, so do it."

"And there will be expenses involved in the cancellation. You've paid deposits, of course, but you can't just leave the people you've hired high and dry. The contracts you signed specify fees in case of a change of plans. I don't have the totals with me, but—"

Anabel laughed. "Oh, really? I'm supposed to pay them for doing nothing? They can get other jobs, if they're as wonderful as you told me they were. Not that it matters—if you think I'm throwing another dime down the drain over this affair, you're wrong. Now get out of my way."

The engine roared, and Kara leaped back just as the BMW shot away, its tires squealing against the concrete drive.

Teaser

1. How does the author contrast the heroine and the "other woman"? What characteristics set the two women apart?

2. How does the author show Anabel's character, rather than telling about her?

3. What attributes show the heroine as a heroic character?

from
The Corporate Wife
(Harlequin Romance®, November 2000)

In this selection from *The Corporate Wife,* the hero, Slater, gives the "other woman" her comeuppance while Erin, the heroine and Slater's personal assistant, stands by in awe.

Despite the coziness of the book-lined walls and the overstuffed furniture, the library felt chilly–a combination, Erin thought, of its windowless position toward the center of the building and the dark, cold glass of the skylight overhead, frosted to provide soft daytime illumination while filtering out the harsh rays which might harm the delicate books. Jessup lit the gas log in the fireplace, and Erin settled contentedly in front of it with her torte, her cup of tea, and a biography of Napoleon which happened to be lying on the floor beside her chair with a slip of paper protruding from chapter twelve.

But it wasn't long before she'd abandoned dessert, drink, and chair to survey the treasures which surrounded her.

She was so absorbed by a case filled with miniature books that she didn't notice the whisper-quiet movement of the pocket doors. Not until she heard Cecile's voice did she look around, and then she realized that she was under the balcony, in the farthest and most shadowed corner of the room, where they might not see her. Even Slater, though he'd asked her to stay, might not realize she was in the library; suggesting she wait there might have been entirely Jessup's idea. Unless one of them spotted her abandoned tea tray...

Cecile flung herself invitingly onto an overstuffed couch. "At least that's finally over," she said. "Call Jessup to get us a drink,

107

darling, and then come here and... relax with me."

Slater closed the library doors. "You've already had plenty to drink, and I'm not interested in relaxing. I asked you to be my hostess, Cecile. When you agreed, you took on certain responsibilities— including, if necessary, concealing your boredom from my guests."

Cecile bristled.

Erin considered knocking a book off the shelf just to let them know she was present, but she suspected that Slater might see damaging a book as a worse sin than mere eavesdropping. She moved out into the light, forgetting the tiny volume she still held in her hands. "Pardon me, I'll just slip out while you—"

Cecile's eyebrows soared. "What's *she* still doing here?"

"That's my business," Slater said crisply, "not yours."

Cecile shook her head, almost sadly. "Slater, you poor innocent, if you can't see what she's up to—"

Erin looked through her and straight at Slater. "If you'll excuse me, sir," she said, "surely whatever it was you wanted to tell me will keep till tomorrow?"

Cecile sniffed.

Slater stepped into Erin's path. "Please wait, Erin. This won't take long." He faced Cecile. "We are not going to sidetrack this conversation by discussing Erin. We're talking about you."

"No, we're not," Cecile said. "You're giving me a lecture, and I won't stand for it. I told you why I was late. I couldn't help it."

"Running into friends is not a good enough excuse. At the least, you owe Erin an apology for having to stand in for you."

Cecile's gaze flicked disdainfully over Erin. "You actually think she minded the chance to play grown-up? Slater, can you really be as naive as you sometimes appear?"

"On the whole," he said, "it's doubtful."

Erin heard the warning in his voice; Cecile apparently didn't, for she went straight on. "You should be glad I agree to put up with these stuffy people for any length of time at all. I've asked you before to invite some of my friends—"

"To provide a contrast?" Slater sounded perfectly polite.

"Naturally. If you're going to expect me to play hostess to this crowd, the least you could do is let me have some interesting people too. Next time—"

"But my dear Cecile," Slater said, "I wouldn't dream of subjecting you to this sort of torture again."

Cecile blinked, and then smiled. "Well, at least you finally understand how much you've been asking of me. And as long as you're flexible about who we invite, of course I'll do my part in return and put up with your business acquaintances once in a while—"

"*We* are not going to be inviting anyone. And you will not be asked to act as hostess here again. Is that clear enough?"

Cecile's jaw dropped. "You're just going to dump me? After all I've—"

"—Invested in trying to capture me?" Slater said. "Please, Cecile, if you must be tedious, go and do it somewhere else." He took two steps toward the fireplace and touched a bell under the mantel. "Jessup will make sure you have cab fare."

Jessup arrived so quickly that Erin couldn't help but wonder whether he'd been hovering in the hallway. She stayed in the shadows as the butler ushered a stone-faced Cecile out. The gas log hissed, but there was no other sound in the room.

Slater was standing very still, one elbow braced on the mantel, staring down at the fire as if he'd just completed the hardest job he'd ever faced.

Erin was startled. She'd never thought of Slater as the tender-hearted sort. Certainly he didn't hesitate when business grew cut-throat, and he was not inclined to mince words, no matter whose feelings might be hurt in the process. Besides, so far as Erin could see, Cecile didn't have any feelings to hurt.

She was surprised—given Cecile's bad behavior—that it had apparently taken so much resolve for Slater to give the woman her comeuppance. But why else would he be staring at the fire as if he was looking at eternity—and not liking what he saw?

Teaser

1. What characteristics set the two women, Erin and Cecile, apart?

2. How does the author show the sort of person the "other woman" is?

3. What attributes show the heroine as a heroic character?

Naming the Baby
(And Everyone Else, Too)

Naming characters can be a very important part of developing their personalities. The first question, of course, is whether the name is appropriate for the character. The woman we thought was called Michelle might turn out on further investigation to be the sort who would call herself Mike.

Not only can a character's name help to show what kind of person he or she is, but the name can hint at the character's history and background. The name may even help in a minor way to foreshadow story developments or even to push them along. If a character named Courtney is told that her real father was an attorney, her mother's action in choosing that name takes on new significance and helps to convince her that the story is true.

But there are other reasons besides personality to choose one name over another. Helping the reader to keep the characters separate and straight is one of the biggest considerations.

Unusual names

Unfamiliar names and unusual spellings can make a main character stand out from the crowd, but an unusual name may be more difficult for the reader to recall and place. If you use unusual names for both main characters, you multiply the risk of confusion. If you name your heroine

Jeramie and your hero Devon, the reader will have to stop and think each time she encounters a name, "Now is that the hero or the heroine?"

If you want to name a main character Dakota or Cameron or something you've made up, then choose a name for the other main character which is gender-specific. Make your main characters Dakota and Elizabeth, or Cameron and Joshua, to make it easier on the reader.

For secondary characters, it's generally wise to stick to better known, more common names.

Unisex names

Unless your plot requires that you have names that can be mixed up, avoid using names that can indicate either sex. It's hard to keep straight whether Pat and Chris are male or female, especially if they're minor characters.

Appropriate to the time

The names you choose should be appropriate for the historical period where the story takes place. Hazel or Charlotte would be unusual choices for a contemporary heroine, and the effect on the reader will be to remind her at every turn of the page that this is only a story. But Charlotte would make a great Regency heroine–she'd have been named after Princess Charlotte. A Regency heroine named Montana, however, would be out of place both geographically and chronologically.

How it looks on the page

Think about how a name, or a combination of names, will look on the finished page. Names that rhyme, names that are the same length, names that start with the same combination of letters, and names that are composed of similar-looking letters can be confusing, particularly to a reader who may be consuming the story in snatches. Beth and Seth, even though they start with different letters, look very much alike. Lee and Les are even more difficult to distinguish.

For your main characters, choose names which start with different letters. It's almost a kind of shorthand for the reader.

Heroes' names

It's not a rule, but most romance heroes happen to have short names which start with one of the hard consonants (B, D, G, K. T). The firm sound of the name helps to characterize the hero as a no-nonsense man of action.

Using names

When you're referring to characters in narrative, choose one name or nickname and use it consistently. If we refer to our hero sometimes as Lucius, sometimes as Mr. Cannon, and sometimes as "the professor," the reader is going to become confused about who's who and how many people are involved.

In dialogue, an entirely different rule applies. The doorman will call him Mr. Cannon, his students might call him Professor or Dr. Cannon, and the heroine might call him anything at all (probably starting with "Loose" Cannon and working down from there).

When using multiple viewpoints, each different viewpoint character will refer to another character in one specific way, but that might be different from what another viewpoint character calls her. Elizabeth's brother might think of her as Betsy and refer to her that way not only in his thoughts and his speech but in narrative presented from his point of view. Her best friend might refer to her as Beth. And she might refer to herself as Elizabeth.

Teaser

1. List five masculine names.

2. List five feminine names.

3. What kind of character would each name fit?

Building a Character

Every character has to have good reason for the things he does. People don't act without cause. They are seldom nasty just for the sake of being nasty– even then, there's nearly always an underlying reason that the individual feels justifies his actions.

In general, even a person's most misguided actions result from a deep belief that he or she is doing the right thing, the best thing possible under the circumstances.

So the most important question we can ask about a character is *Why?* Why does he do what he does? Why does he say what he says? Why does he hold the particular set of attitudes he does?

But if we ask that question first, without a base to build on, we're almost sure to come up with a stereotypical and predictable answer.

So we're going to build our character from the ground up, starting with the very basics.

The Characterization Worksheet

What is this person's name?

Why was s/he named that?

Age?   Birthday?

What astrological sign was s/he born under? Does it matter to him/her?

Where does s/he live? (Urban? Small town? Rural?)

Why did s/he choose to live there? Was this geographical location her choice or someone else's?

Does s/he live in an apartment? a house? What architectural style? Did s/he choose the residence, and why?

Does s/he live by himself? with others?

What kind of vehicle does s/he drive?

What are his/her important material possessions?

Give a brief physical description.

What are his/her hobbies?

What kind of music does s/he enjoy?

Does s/he have pets? If not, why not? Would s/he like to have pets?

What are his/her favorite foods & drinks?

If s/he has an unexpected free half-day, how does s/he spend it?

How would a friend describe him/her?

What is his/her education?

What is his/her job?

Is this a long-term career or just a job?

Why did s/he choose that type of work?

How does s/he feel about his work?

What does s/he want to be doing in twenty years?

How does s/he feel about the opposite sex?

Why does s/he feel that way?

Is s/he married? single? divorced?

Does s/he have children?

Does s/he have former lovers?

How would a former date or lover describe him/her?

Who are his/her parents?

Does s/he have brothers and sisters?

Where was s/he born and raised?

How important is the family relationship to him/her?

Who is his/her best friend? Why?

Who is his/her worst enemy? Why?

Which one event in his/her life has made this person what s/he is today?

How does s/he feel about himself?

What trait does s/he have which s/he wants to keep secret from the world?

What does s/he like most about his/her life?

What does s/he dislike most about his/her life?

What one thing would s/he like to change about the world?

What would this person die to defend?

What is his/her most likeable character trait?

What is his/her most unlikable or troublesome character defect?

As the story begins, what is his/her problem?

What does s/he do that makes this problem worse?

Who is this person's love interest?

What is this person's ideal happy ending?

What reaction do you want the reader to have to this person?

Why should the reader care about this person?

Sample Characterization Worksheet

(See page 134 for a selection from *The Playboy Assignment*,
showing Susannah Miller in action.)

What is this person's name? *Susannah Miller*

Why was s/he named that? *Susannah is an old family name—Mayflower vintage.*

Age? *27*   Birthday?   *Late July*

What astrological sign was s/he born under? Does it matter to him/her? *Leo, but she doesn't much care*

Where does s/he live? (Urban? Small town? Rural?) *Chicago, near north side, not far from Lincoln Park*

Why did s/he choose to live there? Was this geographical location her choice or someone else's? *She was born and raised in a wealthy north suburb, so Chicago's her home town. She chooses to stay because of her business and her mother.*

Does s/he live in an apartment? a house? What architectural style? Did s/he choose the residence, and why? *In an apartment, in a boxy apartment complex that's starting to show its age. It's her choice to live there, but her options were constrained by rental prices.*

Creating Romantic Characters

Does s/he live by himself? with others? *By herself. She'd rather have an inexpensive apartment and privacy than have a roommate.*

What kind of vehicle does s/he drive? *An ordinary car, nothing flashy or elaborate or expensive. Reliable. Good gas mileage. Economy is important.*

What are his/her important material possessions? *Pendant watch on a heavy gold chain. Possessions aren't particularly important to her.*

Give a brief physical description.
Tall and slim with long blond hair.

What are his/her hobbies? *She was a dancer and still exercises and does ballet training. She likes to walk through old cemeteries studying stones and deducing facts about the people buried there.*

What kind of music does s/he enjoy? *Classical.*

Does s/he have pets? If not, why not? Would s/he like to have pets? *No. No time, little space in apartment. Works long hours. Would like to have a dog.*

What are his/her favorite foods & drinks?
She's a chocoholic.

If s/he has an unexpected free half-day, how does s/he spend it? *In the past, wandering through cemeteries. Now she's likely to visit her mother– in nursing home.*

How would a friend describe him/her?
She's the visionary, never short of an idea. Though

most of the ideas don't work out, one in ten is brilliant and makes up for the oddities of the other nine.

What is his/her education?
Bachelor's degree in public relations.

What is his/her job? *One of three partners in an all women-public relations firm called Tryad. The other two partners are her best friends.*

Is this a long-term career or just a job? *Career.*

Why did s/he choose that type of work? *Liked the classes she took in advertising and PR, and it fits in well with her creativity—hosts of brilliant ideas.*

How does s/he feel about his work? *Loves most of it.*

What does s/he want to be doing in twenty years? *The same thing as now, only with more stability in the business (it's new and struggling a bit) so she can be more selective about the clients and campaigns she takes on.*

How does s/he feel about the opposite sex? *Men are fine, but she's too busy to worry about them—her obligations leave her with little time and few resources.*

Why does s/he feel that way? *She was disillusioned by an early love.*

Is s/he married? single? divorced? *Single.*

Does s/he have children? *No, but she once told her parents, in a rebellious moment, she was pregnant, and the story's haunted her to the current day.*

Does s/he have former lovers? *They weren't technically lovers, but she was in love with a man she met while she was in college.*

How would a former date or lover describe him/her? *Unforgettable. Despite the fact that he thinks she lied to him and tried to use him, he has never been able to put her out of his mind.*

Who are his/her parents? *Charles and Elspeth Miller. They're the Northbrook Millers–a high-society family.*

Does s/he have brothers and sisters? *No.*

Where was s/he born and raised? *Northbrook, Illinois– expensive suburb of Chicago.*

How important is the family relationship to him/her? *She thought it wasn't important at all, rebelled against her parents, but when her mother became ill Susannah stepped in and has made sure her mother has the care she needs even if Susannah goes without.*

Who is his/her best friend? Why? *Her partners, Kit and Alison, in the PR firm. They work and play together and understand each other–they're closer than sisters.*

Who is his/her worst enemy? Why? *Her own impulses.*

Which one event in his/her life has made this person what s/he is today? *When she was 19, her parents ripped into the man she was dating, telling him how inadequate he was, and Susannah fired back at them by telling them she had to marry Marc because she was pregnant. She wasn't; she and Marc had never been lovers. But he assumed she was pregnant by another man, wouldn't listen, and left her.*

How does s/he feel about himself? *She's come to terms with her impulsiveness and has turned it to her advantage. Has forgiven herself for the pregnancy story, though she still feels sad about it.*

What trait does s/he have which s/he wants to keep secret from the world? *How her impulsiveness led her to throw away something she badly wanted– a relationship with Marc. The fact that her fancy family lost its money, driving her father to suicide and her mother into mental illness.*

What does s/he like most about his/her life? *Her work.*

What does s/he dislike most about his/her life? *Her mother's illness and how it affects her own life, in terms of guilt and money and time.*

What one thing would s/he like to change about the world? *To have her mother be at peace.*

What would this person die to defend? *Her mother's reputation–not because it's important to Susannah but because it was so important to Elspeth.*

What is his/her most likeable character trait? *Humor and her willingness to do anything for the people she loves.*

What is his/her most unlikable or troublesome

character defect? *Acting on impulse.*

As the story begins, what is his/her problem? *Marc has come back into her life, and because of her job she must deal with him or lose an important client.*

What does s/he do that makes this problem worse? *Refuses to answer his questions about the pregnancy story, because she feels it's none of his business any more.*

Who is this person's love interest? *Marc Herrington.*

What is this person's ideal happy ending? *To patch up her romance with Marc, and carry on from a more mature standpoint than either would have been capable of years before.*

What reaction do you want the reader to have to this person? *Liking, affection, amusement.*

Why should the reader care about this person? *She's a likeable individual caught in a situation anyone can understand, because we've all said things on impulse that we regretted, and had to face the consequences.*

Teaser

Look at each of the illustrations on the following pages and use the questions in the characterization worksheet to learn about each person or situation. Then write a few sentences about each character. What is this person like? What has happened in his life to make him this way?

127

Who is this man?
the heroine's father?
her boss?
her favorite uncle?

Is this man the hero?
the hero's good friend?
the heroine's brother?
the man she was dating
when she met the hero?

Who is this woman?
the heroine?
her good friend?
someone the hero
used to date?

Is this woman the heroine?
the hero's sister?
a friend from work?
her next-door neighbor?

If one of these women was the heroine and one the "other woman," which one would you choose for which role? Why?

Who is this child?
the heroine's daughter?
the hero's?
the child of a friend or
  relative, and they're
  babysitting for
  the weekend?

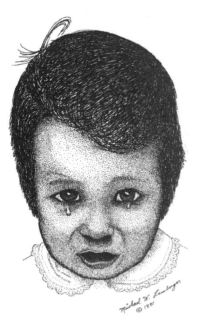

What has caused
the tears?

130

Bringing Characters to Life

The best way to reveal characters is to show them in action. Let what they say and do (and think, if they're POV characters) tell the reader about them. And don't forget that what they *don't* say and *don't* do— for instance, if they restrain themselves from being rude even when they're being baited— can tell just as much about them as what they say and do. The least effective way to show a character is to describe him. Straight narration doesn't hold the reader's attention for long.

So instead of writing, "Sally was a kind, polite person," show how she treats the gum-chewing teenager who messes up her order at McDonalds. Contrasting what she says and does with what she thinks can be very effective.

Here are the main ways in which we can show a character:

Through the character's own thoughts.

The way our minds work illustrates the kind of people we are. If a character thinks about another character's difficulty with sympathy and compassion, the reader will get the message.

Through the character's own words.

What a person says about his actions, intentions, and history— and whether what he says matches reality— can be very revealing of his character.

Through the character's own actions.

If he draws back a fist to hit a child, he's painted himself as a villain no matter what he says.

Through another character's thoughts.

This technique should be limited to the point of view of major characters or we risk taking the emphasis off the main story. We might get the heroine's thoughts about her hairdresser; we aren't likely to get the hairdresser's thoughts about the heroine.

Through another character's words.

What one person says about another can't always be taken at face value, but whether it's true or not, the reader will get a better picture of both the speaker and the subject.

Through another character's actions.

If a character walks through a room and the dog cringes to get out of his way, it's pretty clear what kind of person we're dealing with.

Through physical description.

This is probably the most-used (especially by inexperienced writers) and one of the least-effective techniques. It's particularly useless when couched in generalities like "She was beautiful"– because that phrase means very different things to different people.

Through habits or individual traits.

More easily used to illustrate unlikable characteristics than good ones. A man who issues a lunch invitation and then dodges the check creates a lasting impression.

Through the props that surround the character.

What a character chooses to surround himself with gives the reader a view of what kind of person he is. Does he walk into the room carrying a tennis racquet? a handgun? a Bible?

Through the character's name.

A man named Sylvester creates an entirely different impression than one called Jake. A woman named Kim is a whole different creature than one named Sabrina. Does the name you've chosen fit the personality you're depicting?

Through narrative description. Simply stating the character type and traits, without showing examples of behavior, words, or thoughts to illustrate the statement, is less effective because it requires the reader to accept the author's judgment rather than making her own.

Teaser

1. Think about a character you have enjoyed reading about. How does the author show you what kind of a person the character is?

from
The Playboy Assignment
(Harlequin Romance®, April 1998)

In this opening scene from The Playboy Assignment, we meet heroine Susannah Miller (see the characterization worksheet example starting on page 121) and one of her partners in the public relations firm where she works.

The scent of freshly made coffee filled the small café, and Susannah paused in the doorway for a second to breathe her fill of the rich aroma. But one of her partners was already waiting in the back booth they reserved by their staff meeting every Monday morning, so Susannah strolled down the length of the long, narrow room and sat across from Alison.

She winced at the hardness of the green vinyl bench. "I'm either going to have to start carrying along a cushion or convince the management to redecorate."

Alison folded her newspaper and laid it aside. "The cushion would be easier. This place has looked the same as long as I can remember. So unless you're looking for a challenge—"

"Any reason I shouldn't be?" Susannah poured herself a cup of coffee from the carafe on the table.

"Only that redecorating isn't really a matter of public relations."

Susannah squirmed on the bench. "I don't know about that. My particular segment of the public would have a lot better relations with the management if—"

"*And* we've already got plenty of regular business to tend to.

Which forces me to point out that you're late." Alison's tone was matter-of-fact, without a hint of reproach or irritation.

Susannah reached automatically for the pendant watch which dangled from a heavy gold chain around her neck. "Five minutes," she said. "And I'd have been smack on time if there hadn't been a bake sale going on outside the high school as I walked past."

Alison showed faint interest. "And this hour on a Monday morning?"

"Incredible, isn't it? I thought any teenager who was enterprising enough to be selling brownies this early deserved my support." She pulled a paper bag from her briefcase and waved it under Alison's nose. "So I bought both fudge and chocolate-chip cookies—but you can't have any till after breakfast."

The waitress set an omelette in front of Alison and grinned at Susannah. "What'll it be this morning, Sue?"

"Just a raspberry Danish. No hurry."

Alison picked up her fork. "Better make it bacon and eggs instead of more sugar, or you'll be bouncing off the walls by noon. Not that you don't most of the time, anyway."

"I didn't buy *that* much fudge." There was no defensiveness in Susannah's tone; Alison's comment was too near truth to allow room for resentment. Of the three partners in Tryad Public Relations, Alison was the practical manager, Kit was the steady get-it-done-whatever-it-takes sort, and Susannah was the visionary, never short of an idea.

The fact that nine out of ten of those ideas went nowhere had ceased to bother her—because the tenth was always a winner.

Of course, that had been true all her life. For every good plan she'd ever come up with, Susannah Miller had managed to find nine bad ones. Or sometimes, she thought dryly, an idea so far beyond bad that it was worth nine all by itself. That whole thing with Marc—

And that, Susannah told herself, was enough of that. Marc

and the last of her disasters were eight long years in the past, and there was no point in rehashing the circumstances. The important thing was with two down-to-earth partners to keep her anchored to reality, her wilder ideas were squashed *before* they could get her into trouble.

(Though this selection establishes Susannah's habit of impulsive action and wild ideas, the reader doesn't find out exactly what Susannah's "idea so far beyond bad that it was worth nine all by itself" was until almost 175 pages later.)

(*The Playboy Assignment* is the second book of the **Finding Mr. Right** trilogy. The other two titles are *The Billionaire Date* and *The Husband Project*.)

Teaser

1.   What methods are used to illustrate the character of the heroine?

2. What methods are used to illustrate the other characters?

3. What information from the characterization worksheet is included in the first few pages of the book? What information is left out?

from
Let Me Count the Ways
(Harlequin Romance®, December 1989)

In this selection, hero and thriller-writer Adam Merrill becomes a houseguest in the home of heroine Sara Prentiss's elderly friend, Olivia, and–after sneaking a kiss from Sara– begins inquiring into the long-ago disappearance of Olivia's daughter Pamela.

Adam reached for the suitcase on the floor at her feet and set it on the other twin bed. He had efficiently unpacked half of it before Sara felt she could trust her voice again. *You idiot,* she told herself. *You're jumping at shadows! Just pretend the whole thing never happened, and go back to treating him the way you did before.*

"Is there a picture of Pamela anywhere in the house?" he asked her suddenly.

"Not that I've ever seen." She watched as he took a ceramic mug full of pens and pencils out of a plastic bag and set it on the corner of the small desk. The mug was chipped and battered, as if it had been carried around the world.

"Not even in Olivia's room?'

"And just what excuse would you have for being in Olivia's room?" she asked tartly. "Surely you're going to stop fooling around with the thing about Pamela, aren't you, now that you're living here? Out of courtesy to your hostess, Adam– "

"The rules of etiquette say that a guest should do whatever he can to make his hostess's life more pleasant, and if that means solving her mystery– "

"It could get a little nasty," Sara pointed out, "if a skeleton falls out of a closet that you're not supposed to be poking around in."

He frowned. "I see your point. All right I'll think about it, Sara."

She supposed she would have to be content with that. He took a silver picture frame from the suitcase and set it on the corner of the desk. "There," he said. "That makes it begin to feel like home."

She had caught a glimpse of the photograph, of a smiling family. *I'm amazed that it isn't a glamorous solo portrait of a lady wearing feathers,* she thought. *Or a police evidence shot of a bleeding corpse – either of those would seem to be much more likely than a family photo to get a spot on Adam's desk!* "Do you carry around everything you possess?"

"No, but I travel a lot. A few familiar things make a great deal of difference."

Sara let out a gleeful shriek. "Things like this?" She pounced on a small fuzzy item in the bottom corner of the suitcase and held it up.

"Sara, that is personal property!"

"I should say it's personal, So you're human after all," she announced, fighting off a case of the giggles. She collapsed into a chair and held the small stuffed dog out at arm's length. "Do you have to cuddle up with him to get to sleep after you write all that nonsense about torture and mayhem?"

Adam sighed. "No, I'm not troubled with insomnia, and I don't cuddle him as I go to sleep. Though if you're offering your services as a substitute, I'm sure I could get use to cuddling you."

Sara ignored him. "Do you know what a gossip column item this would make?" she jeered. "Famous macho author travels with stuffed dog. What's his name?"

"Buddy." He looked a bit put out, she thought, as if he'd like to grab the animal back from her and hide it. No wonder, she thought.

How perfectly embarrassing for him to be caught with a childhood toy.

"Oh, I see now," she said. "It's sewn on his collar. I suppose you got him when you were a baby."

"I've always had him."

"He's practically antique."

"Thanks," Adam said drily.

"And he's almost worn out, too." She inspected the dog. His ears flopped disreputably over his face. One beady eye had been replaced by a button, and his tail looked as if it had been chewed. His stuffing had shifted here and there, leaving one of Buddy's front legs too limp to hold his weight. When Sara set him down on the bed, he toppled over with his nose resting against the dark blue bedspread.

She picked him up again and put him on a shelf above the desk, propping him securely between two books. "There," she said. "He can keep you company while you work and guard you while you sleep."

Adam was watching her thoughtfully, his arms folded across his chest. "At least he seems to have restored your good mood."

"Of course," Sara said cheerfully. "Haven't you figured that out? It makes us even, you see — now I've got blackmail material too!"

Teaser

1. How is the reader shown Adam's character? Sara's?

2. What do Adam's personal possessions reveal about him?

3. What do you know (and not know) about each character?

from
A Matter of Principal
(Harlequin Romance® August 1990)

In this scene, we get to know the three main characters– hero, heroine, and the child who is the significant third character– as the heroine struggles to keep her bed-and-breakfast business from being repossessed by the bank, represented by the hero.

Camryn didn't sleep well, of course, and when the alarm clock gave its characteristic asthmatic wheeze, as it always did just before shrieking at her, she was already sitting on the edge of her bed with her hand on the button. She yawned and went to push aside the curtains. The pair of dormer windows in her bedroom looked out over the front of the house, towards the rising sun. Today, unfortunately, there was no sun to see–just the dim gray softness of a summer rainstorm, blurring the outlines of the world.

Camryn sighed and pulled her cotton nightshirt over her head. No comfortable shorts and sandals today, or battered, soft jeans, either. She wasn't going to face another one of those contemptuous looks from Mrs. Marlow if she could help it.

The sound of the shower woke Susan, who wandered in while Camryn was getting dressed and sat cross-legged on the big bed, clutching her ragged teddy bear. "Ipswich is lonely shut up in Sherry's room," she announced. "I can hear him. Can I go play with him?"

"Not till Sherry wakes up. And it's Saturday, so it might be a while." Sherry's young man from the university library had come by last night as promised, and they had gone to one of the campus coffee-houses. Camryn didn't even know what time Sherry had come home; she herself had not gone to sleep till after midnight, but it wasn't unusual for Sherry to arrive with the morning newspaper.

"Stupid Mrs. Marlow," Susan grumbled. "Ipswich doesn't like to be shut up."

"That's quite enough, Susan. You have a right to like cats; other people have a right not to. And, whether we agree with them or not, we have to treat our guests with respect."

Privately, Camryn agreed with her; Mrs. Marlow alone was an aggravating as three ordinary guests, and so far she hadn't earned much respect. Thank heaven, Camryn thought, that she would be spending much of her time this weekend with her son, away from the Stone House. He'd be picking her up in a couple of hours, right after she had her breakfast—in bed, as she'd requested. And if it wasn't delivered to her door on the dot of the hour, there would be trouble. It didn't take a crystal ball to foresee that.

Camryn tied her hair back with a silk scarf that matched her slim, high-waisted trousers and said, "Come on, Susan. You can help me make Danish."

Outside, the clouds rumbled and the rain fell softly, but the two of them worked companionably in the brightly lit kitchen, Camryn shaping the soft, cheese-filled dough into circles, and Susan topping each pastry with strawberry jam. Her spoonfuls were sometimes uncertain, and their placement approximate at best, but she was having a great deal of fun. *Besides,* thought Camryn, *we can pick out the best-looking two for Mrs. Marlow, and eat the irregular ones ourselves.*

When the doorbell chimed just as the first pan of Danish went into the oven, Camryn felt something very near panic. It can't be that late, she thought. Unless the rainstorm knowcked out the power last night, and made my clocks all wrong...

But it wasn't John Marlow who had rung the bell. For an instant as she opened the door she thought she was imagining things. Surely it wasn't really Patrick McKenna, standing in a puddle on her front porch, with his hair so wet that it was plastered flat against his head? He was wiping raindrops off his face...

"You're soaked." *That was a stupid thing to say,* she told herself. *The important thing is, he's here. He didn't give up on me after all. But on Saturday? At this hour?*

"There was a damned cloudburst the instant I got out of the car," he growled.

"Glad you enjoyed it," Camryn murmured. "I arranged it on purpose just for your entertainment."

He stared at her for an instant and then started to laugh. It was a very pleasant sound, she thought. He ought to do it more often.

"Come in," she said. "Make yourself at home. Drip wherever you like. I'm a bit busy with breakfast at the moment, so if you'd like a cup of coffee in the living room while you wait—"

"Can I watch instead?" He sounded almost like Susan for an instant.

It caught her off guard, and she smiled at him almost as she would have at the child. "Sure you can."

It wasn't until they got to the kitchen that it occurred to her why he was so interested. *Of course,* she thought. *He wants to see how things operate, and if I really am as disorganized as I looked yesterday.*

Susan was standing on a chair beside the center island, absorbed in decorating the second panful of Danish. She was working earnestly, her tongue stuck out in concentration, and she didn't even look up as they came in. Camryn took one look at the pan and said, "Susan, a spoonful, for heaven's sake! You don't cover the whole top of the Danish—"

"But I like a lot of jam," Susan said reasonably. Her eyes fell on the man following her mother.

"So do I," he confided. "We didn't really get a chance to meet yesterday, did we, Susan?"

"You're all wet," she said.

"One thing about the Hastings women," he muttered. "They're observant."

Camryn handed him a towel. "This is Mr. McKenna, Susan."

Susan tried the name out, and stumbled over her tongue. Patrick McKenna leaned over the island and held out his hand. "How about calling me Patrick?" he said. "It'll be easier."

Susan grinned at him and licked a spot of strawberry jam off her palm before putting her sticky little hand into his. He didn't flinch.

That's just great, Camryn thought. *Obviously her shyness yesterday was a fluke because she was so tired. Now my daughter is on a first-name basis with the man who's going to throw us out of our house... That's not fair,* she reminded herself. *After all, he did say he'd help.*

Teaser

1. What methods are used to show the characters?

2. How do the interactions of the characters show what kind of people they are?

3. By the end of the scene, what do we know about each of the three characters? What don't we know about the characters?

The Pursuit of Love

Remember the definition of the romance novel? It's the story of a man and a woman who, *while they're solving a problem*, fall in love.

That problem can't be simply, Is this the person I want to spend the rest of my life with? It needs to be more complex than that, for this background, the difficulties which surround this couple falling in love at this moment, is what makes the romance novel exciting.

So in addition to the attraction between the main characters, there must be some issue to be sorted out, some problem to be solved, some disagreement to be settled during the course of the story.

That problem threatens to prevent our heroic couple from discovering and acting on their once-in-a-lifetime love. It does this not just because it's a nuisance, but because this particular difficulty creates conflict and tension between the two of them.

Teaser

In romances you've read recently, what problems do the hero and heroine face?

Problems and Solutions

All stories are about problems– characters facing difficulties and solving (or not solving) them. The romance novel is no exception, though unlike in some literary fiction the problem is always resolved at the end of the romance novel.

A character with a problem is an interesting character. Trouble for the character means tension, excitement and interest for the reader. But that doesn't necessarily mean that the more troubles we throw at the character, the better. If we have our heroine fall out of a tree, then get hit by a car, then encounter a rattlesnake, we're not creating a plot; we're grabbing at straws.

The most absorbing problems are ones which develop, grow, change, and become more complicated, creating new problems and more trouble for the characters. In other words, we're looking for one main problem which has the potential to get even worse as the story progresses.

Misunderstandings and arguments

A simple misunderstanding is not a problem. If two people sitting down for an honest five-minute discussion could solve the difficulty, that's not enough of a conflict to keep a book going, no matter how many cute tricks the author creates to keep the couple from having that five-minute chat.

Arguments aren't the same as problems, either.

People can be strongly opposed to each other without ever raising their voices. But it's equally true that they can argue loudly, incessantly, and pointlessly– never addressing an important issue. Having a hero and heroine who can't agree about anything– and who make no bones about saying so– isn't the same as giving them a problem to confront.

Situations

A problem that doesn't have potential for developing and getting worse is only a situation. If our heroine is rock-climbing and falls off a cliff, that's not a plot-producing problem, it's only a single event– a situation. Either she'll be rescued or she'll die and either case the story is over.

Falling off a cliff can form the basis of a plot, however, if we look a little further. Instead of having her fall off, let's just leave her stranded– stuck halfway up, with no way to get up or down. Now that's a problem that get can worse.

The effective problem

But even more important, let's ask why she's on the cliff in the first place. That's where the real potential for problems lies. Is she trying to protect the secret microfilm she's carrying from the bad guys who are chasing her? Is she learning to climb because the man she thinks she loves wants her to share his mountain-climbing hobby?

The most effective problem is one that is particularly important to these characters. Getting stuck on a cliff wouldn't be pleasant for anybody, but it would be horrible for a character who had a fear of heights, or who was lost in the mountains when she was a child, or whose mother died when she fell off a rock-climbing wall at the gym.

146

It's even better if the problem is especially thorny for both characters. The fact that our heroine is afraid of heights wouldn't make a great deal of difference to most men. But if our hero is a climbing instructor, or if he personally builds skyscrapers, her fear will have much more impact on his life.

Bad for each other

Some of the most interesting problems are ones in which the hero and heroine seem to be the worst possible combination. He's the last man on earth she should be falling in love with, and vice-versa.

If our heroine's father was a compulsive gambler who died broke and left his family in poverty, but the hero runs a string of casinos... If the heroine has never had a real home, but now that she's finally got one the hero's bought the building and is going to tear it down... If marriage and stability are critical to the heroine, but the hero's just had an infant son from a previous casual relationship dumped on his doorstep...

Those couples are facing big trouble.

Working together

Another effective type of story problem requires the couple to cooperate to solve a difficulty. This may be one problem which affects them both, or it can be a trade– she needs something he can provide, but he'll do her a favor only if in return she gives him what he needs.

If the hero's father and the heroine's mother announce they're getting married, but the hero and heroine think the two older people would be awful for each other, they'll try their collective best to stop the wedding. If the heroine and hero each have a claim to an orphaned baby, they'll try to figure out a way for both to have custody.

If the heroine inherits something that should have gone to the hero, she may be willing to give it back only if he'll help her out of a sticky situation at work. If the hero wants a pretend engagement to protect him from a carnivorous woman who won't take no for an answer, the heroine may be willing to cooperate– in return for money to take care of her sick father.

Solving the problem

Whatever the problem is, it's important to remember the rule that it will have to be resolved in the end.

Perhaps one of the main characters has an epiphany that changes his or her feelings (our rock-climbing heroine confronts her fear of heights and overcomes it). Or one of them makes a sacrifice in order to please the other (our casino-running hero sells out and buys a department store instead). Or they compromise (he tears down her house after all, but salvages all the important pieces so he can build her a new and better home).

What kind of problem will be large enough to create real disagreement between your main characters for the entire length of the book, and yet will allow them to find a solution or a compromise which will satisfy them both?

What kind of solution will achieve your happy ending without being so obvious to the reader that your heroic couple look like fools for not thinking of it immediately?

Teaser

Make a list of problems a hero or heroine might face.

from
Bride by Design
(Harlequin Romance®, November 2002)

In this selection from the first chapter of *Bride by Design*, the heroine's grandfather, Henry Birmingham, has offered the hero a business deal. If he agrees to the conditions, David will eventually own Henry's business, a famous Chicago jewelry store known as Birmingham on State. But there are some strings attached which affect not only David but the heroine, Eve.

Henry had been gone for a full quarter of an hour when David's head finally stopped thrumming and he could begin to think straight again.

It isn't Henry Birmingham who's gone around the bend, Elliot—it's you.

What in hell had he agreed to do, he asked himself in despair. And why?—though that was a foolish question. Dangling Birmingham on State in front of him had been like tantalizing a shark with a big chunk of raw tuna, and Henry had known it. Though it actually wasn't the business itself that David had snapped at, tempting though it was. It was the freedom Henry had offered, a freedom that he chafed for and knew that he would never find unless he could be his own boss.

The man was a mesmerist, that was the only explanation. Henry had hypnotized him into thinking that the offer he had made was feasible, when in fact...

He should get out right now, while he still could. Stand up and walk out of the little tavern. Hail the first cab he saw and get himself to O'Hare and onto the next plane back to Atlanta. Shake the dust of the Windy City off his feet and never look back.

But he didn't move.

Birmingham on State. Handed to him on a platter...with a few conditions, of course.

Conditions that *she*—Henry's granddaughter—would never agree to.

An odd mixture of disappointment and relief trickled through him. He didn't have to walk out, he thought. He could sit here and wait for half an hour, just as he'd promised Henry he would. And when she didn't show up—well, he'd have done his best, wouldn't he? and Henry couldn't blame him.

David checked his watch. Twenty minutes had gone already. All he had to do was wait another ten, and it would be over.

But he had to admit to a pang. Birmingham on State... For a few brief, brilliant moments, he had hoped. He had seen a vision of the wonders he could create—if only he had the freedom and the opportunity and the backing.

A low voice spoke beside him. "David Elliot?"

He looked up almost hopefully, expecting the waitress. Perhaps Henry's granddaughter had at least called the tavern and sent him a message to say she wasn't coming. It would be the decent thing to do, instead of leaving him dangling. It wasn't as if he was to blame for her grandfather's crazy ideas, after all.

But the woman who stood beside the booth wasn't wearing the tavern's uniform. She was dressed in a dark green suit that hugged her in all the right spots, and a string of perfectly-matched pearls peeked out from inside the high collar of her jacket, right at the base of her throat. She was small-boned and petite. Her face was heart-shaped, her eyes as green as the suit and fringed with the darkest lashes he'd ever seen, and her pure-black hair was drawn back into a loose knot at the nape of her neck.

"My grandfather sent me," she said.

David felt as if someone had plunged a very sharp, very thin knife into the sensitive spot just beneath his ribs. He didn't know what he'd expected Henry Birmingham's granddaughter to be like—in fact, he'd had no expectations, for he hadn't given the matter an instant's conscious thought. He only knew that this woman wasn't anything like he would have anticipated. This woman would turn heads in a morgue.

She said, "He suggested we chat over lunch."

David scrambled to get to his feet, belatedly trying to at least look like a gentleman. "You're... Eve," he said, and felt as foolish as he must have sounded.

"Yes. Eve Birmingham." Her gaze was as direct and intent as Henry's, her eyes as bright and searching. But her face was curiously still. "May I?" Without waiting for an answer, she slid into the seat across from him.

David was glad he could sit down again himself, for his knees had gone a little weak. He had never dreamed she would actually come...

Just because she's here doesn't mean she's agreeable, he reminded himself. *She might just be too polite to leave me stranded. Or maybe she doesn't even suspect what Henry's got in mind.*

Eve asked the waitress to bring her a pot of tea, and David used the interval to collect himself.

"I understand you and Henry have had a heart-to-heart talk," she said as she filled her cup.

"He had some interesting proposals," David said, and caught himself. *Bad choice of words, Elliot.* "I mean... Look, I don't know if he's told you what this is all about."

Eve set the teapot down. "Henry keeps very few secrets from me."

"This may be one of them."

"I've known for quite a while that he was thinking about

retiring, and that he didn't want to sell the business and take the chance that it would become something less than what he's worked so hard to maintain. He told me some time ago that he was looking for a young designer, an artisan who shared his vision of what jewelry could be, to carry on for him."

"What about you?" David didn't realize until the words were out that the question had been nagging at him ever since Henry had made his crazy offer. "Don't you want the job?"

Eve shrugged. "I know good design when I see it, but I could no more produce it myself than I can fly to the moon. Those genes passed me by."

"You sound very calm about it."

"I've had years to come to terms with the idea that my talents run in other directions. So has Henry, as a matter of fact—he realized long since that I wasn't able to be quite what he needed."

"But you must have feelings about him bringing a stranger in."

"Of course I do. As a matter of fact, I'm very involved in the business—I manage the staff, I handle customer service, I watch the bottom line. But I have to agree with Henry. Much as it would hurt me to close down Birmingham on State, I'd rather see that happen than have it be merged into one of the companies that mass-produces jewelry for the lowest common denominator." She looked at him across her tea cup. "If he thinks you're the right man, then I'm quite happy to endorse his choice."

David rubbed his knuckles against his jaw. "If you're serious about that, then he can't have told you his whole plan." He poured himself more coffee. He'd had too much already, he knew. His nerves were jangling. On the other hand, that would probably be happening even if he hadn't consumed any caffeine at all.

Her voice was calm. "If you're asking whether he's confided in me that he wants me to marry his chosen successor—"

152

David dropped his spoon. "You know about that, too?"

The look she gave him was almost sad. "I did tell you that he keeps very few things from me."

"You can say that again. You must think it's a little medieval of him."

She looked as if she was thinking it over. "He has his reasons," she said finally. "His own marriage was arranged by his family, and it was successful—so of course the idea occurred to him when he began thinking of the future of Birmingham on State. Legal partnerships have their shortcomings, while a marriage would be safer for the business. A stranger who marries into the family isn't a stranger any more. I couldn't toss you out on your ear if you displeased me, but you couldn't take over the firm and cut me out, either."

"He obviously hasn't heard about this thing called divorce."

"He sees no reason why a marriage which is arranged to achieve good and sensible goals, and entered into with both parties' full knowledge and agreement, should ever dissolve. And I must say I agree."

"My God, you don't only look like the ice queen, you're frozen all the way through."

The words were out before he'd stopped to think, and for an instant he thought he saw the glint of tears in Eve's eyes before she looked away. Regret surged through him. It wasn't like him to be carelessly rude.

But before he could speak, she'd faced him again, and her gaze was resolute. "Of course, you should also understand that Henry is looking to the future of Birmingham on State. Beyond his lifetime—but also beyond yours and mine. A legal partnership can't create an heir for the business, but a marriage could."

The woman was obviously serious. *Along with being crazy as a loon,* he thought. He set his cup down with a click. "And you still don't think he's a little twisted?"

Eve's voice was cool. "I think that what Henry doesn't know won't hurt him."

"In other words," David said slowly, "whatever Henry has in mind, you're planning on a marriage in name only."

She nodded.

"Why?"

Her composure seemed to slip. "You mean why don't I want to... to—"

"No, I'm not asking why you don't want to sleep with me. I want to know why you'd settle for a marriage that isn't a marriage."

Her fingers tightened on her cup till her knuckles were white. But her voice was once more steady. "I don't think that's any of your business. Let's just say that I have my reasons for wanting the protection of a wedding ring, without emotional entanglements."

You poor deluded darling, he thought. *To think that a ring will keep men from hitting on you, the way you look...* Of course, once a man actually got close enough to realize that underneath the gorgeous, intriguing exterior lay the soul of a glacier, he probably wouldn't come back for more. But there would always be another man in line...

Then her words echoed oddly through his mind. *I have my reasons for wanting the protection of a wedding ring.*

"I think I see," he said gently. "You may as well tell me, Eve. Do you know that you're pregnant or are you just afraid you might be?"

She drew in a sharp breath and for a moment he thought she was going to throw her tea cup at him. He watched with fascination as the color rose in her cheeks, as she fought for and regained self-control. So she wasn't quite as chilly as she'd seemed; the glacier appeared to have a crack or two.

"Neither," she snapped.

"That's good. I've never given much thought to the idea of raising kids, but I guess if I was stuck with a couple of rug rats I'd rather they be mine."

He could almost hear the tinkle of ice in her voice. "You certainly won't have to worry about rug rats."

"You're pretty certain I'm going to agree to this crazy plan."

"It would be very foolish of you to walk away. To be Henry Birmingham's hand-picked successor is a solid-gold opportunity."

"I wonder what he'd do if I turned him down," David mused.

Eve shrugged. "Probably work his way on through his list."

"What list?" He recalled a comment Henry had made almost carelessly. At the time David been too flattered by the idea that the king of jewelry design had noticed him at all to pay much attention to the details. But suddenly he remembered the remark all too well. Henry hadn't just told David he was talented. He'd said something about him being one of the three best young designers in the country. So Henry had a list of three...at least.

Eve's gaze flicked over him. "Don't take it personally. You can't think you're the only gifted young man in the country. Or that Henry would gamble the future of his business on the first man who seemed to meet his specifications, without looking any further."

"How far down his list was I?"

"I don't know exactly." Her voice was calm and level.

"I see. That's one of the few things he didn't share with you."

"Quite right. If it makes you feel any better, you're the first one he's asked me to meet."

So if there had been others higher on Henry's list, they hadn't passed all the hidden tests along the way. "That's a relief. I think."

"Anyway, now that he's made the offer, it doesn't matter where you ranked. Any designer with sense wouldn't worry about how his number happened to come up, he'd gladly give an arm for this opportunity."

"Actually," David mused. "You're wrong about that. Henry isn't asking for an arm—just a rib."

She fidgeted with her tea cup, turning it round and round on the saucer. "As far as that goes," she said. Her voice was different, almost hesitant, and he was intrigued. "I don't expect there would be much contact, really. We'd have to share a house, I suppose."

"I think Henry would notice if we were living in separate suburbs, yes."

"But I don't see any reason why we couldn't be civil about it."

"Roommates," he said thoughtfully.

"If you want to put it that way. And what he's asking is nothing, really, weighed against Birmingham on State."

It all came back to the business, David knew. Eve was absolutely right. Henry Birmingham's offer presented a chance he could never have achieved on his own. It was an opportunity he could not refuse, whatever the cost—because to turn it down would be to sacrifice his dreams and throw away his talent. There would never be another opening like this.

He looked across the table at her and felt his future shift—as if he had slid into some kind of time warp—and settle into a new pattern. A pattern that included Birmingham on State. And Eve.

"Let's have lunch," he said, "and plan a wedding."

Teaser

1. What is David's problem at the start of the story?

2. What is Eve's problem?

3. How do the problems fit together?

4. How might the problems grow worse?

5. How might the problems eventually be solved?

Creating Romantic Characters

from
The Tycoon's Baby
(Harlequin Romance®, October 1999)

In these two scenes from the first chapter of *The Tycoon's Baby*, we see hero Webb Copeland and heroine Janey Griffin separately. Each faces a problem– Webb has a matchmaking grandmother, Janey has taken on more than she can handle between college and a job. But before long the two will be unlikely– and yet perfect– allies.

The room rang with the sound of a toddler's giggles. Webb raised himself up on one elbow and leaned over the pajama-clad child who was sprawled on the Oriental rug in front of the fireplace. He growled gently as he threatened once more to gobble her tummy, and she shrieked with delight and yanked at his hair.

Nearby, a white-uniformed woman shifted to the edge of her chair and said, "Mr. Copeland, it's Madeline's bedtime."

Who cares? Webb wanted to say. *I don't, and Madeline certainly doesn't.* "I've only seen my little girl for twenty minutes all day, Mrs. Wilson. Can't her bedtime be put off for a while?"

The nurse's expression was stern. "I'd say you've already managed that. You've got her so agitated it'll take an hour just to get her settled."

Webb sighed and made a vow to himself that tomorrow he *would* get out of the office on time, no matter what. "All right." He bent over the toddler again. "Maddy, playtime's over. Give me a kiss before you go up to bed."

Madeline's enormous brown eyes—her mother's eyes—

pleaded silently, but Webb gathered her close and stood up. He rubbed his cheek against her soft dark hair and kissed her rosy cheek, then handed her over to the nurse and watched the pair of them cross the marble-tiled foyer and climb the winding stairs.

The tiny woman perched on a low rocking chair at one side of the fireplace didn't look up from the mass of rose-colored yarn in her lap. The flicker of the flames cast long shadows which emphasized the deep lines etched in her face. "I don't know why you put up with that woman, Webb."

"Because she's the best baby nurse in Cook County."

Camilla Copeland sniffed. "Says who?"

"She was highly recommended."

"She's rigid."

"Gran, you can't have it both ways. I've heard you say yourself that children need schedules."

"I said they need security and stability. That does not mean I'm in favor of regimentation."

Webb buttoned the collar of his pinstriped shirt and settled his tie back into place. "Gran, please don't start this again." But he might as well have tried to stop a battleship.

"Madeline's only fifteen months old. Don't you think it's a bit early for her to be living a boarding school lifestyle, all bells and whistles and rules?" Camilla Copeland looked straight at her grandson and added firmly, "The child needs a mother."

Webb dropped into a chair. He might as well make himself as comfortable as possible. They'd had this discussion a dozen times at least, and he knew better than to think he could cut it short now, because, once launched, Camilla was inexorable.

Her voice softened. "I know it affected you horribly, when Sibyl... went—"

"You have no idea, Gran."

"But it's been more than a year since she died, and it's time for you to get on with your life."

"I *am* getting on with my life. What I don't plan to do is get married again—ever."

"Oh, my dear." Camilla's voice was soft. "I know that you've been stunned—almost in a daze—ever since the accident. But you mustn't assume that because you haven't felt any interest in women in this past year that you never will. Those... urges... aren't gone, Webb."

Despite his annoyance with her, Webb had to bite back a laugh. Dear old Gran, with her Victorian way of putting things! She'd even turned just a little pink, bless her heart. Or was that simply the firelight reflecting off the half-finished sweater in her lap?

Camilla turned her knitting and started another row. "Someday, Webb, I promise you'll be eager to have a woman in your life again."

Webb wondered what she'd say if he pointed out that he'd only ruled out marriage, not the possibility of another woman in his life.

"And it'll be easier for Madeline to accept a stepmother now than it will be later." Camilla nodded firmly, as if she'd nailed her point and was assured there could be no argument.

Webb blinked in surprise. He'd thought he could practically recite this entire conversation from beginning to end with all its variations, but that last line had been a completely new twist. He felt like a skier who'd wandered off the marked trail and found himself speeding down the side of an entirely different mountain.

"Now wait a minute," he said. "Because you're so certain that someday I'll decide to get married again, you think I should leap into it right now—whether I'm ready or not—because Maddy's the right age to bond with a stepmother?"

"I didn't say you should leap," Camilla said. "I said you shouldn't write off the possibility."

Webb shook his head. "No, you weren't nearly that flexible, Gran. So let's assume I take your advice and get married, against my better judgment, purely so Maddy can have a stepmother—"

"I never indicated that you should consider only what's best for Madeline. I expect you'd have a few criteria of your own."

"That's very generous of you," Webb said with mock humility. "I'm grateful to have a say in this."

"Don't be impudent, Webb." Camilla pushed her knitting needles deep into the mass of pink yarn. "There's the bell, and we won't be able to finish this discussion over dinner."

Because the butler would hear, Webb thought. *Thank heaven for small blessings.*

"But I want your promise that you'll think it over."

Webb offered his arm. "I assure you, Gran," he said gravely, "that I'll give the idea all the consideration it deserves."

Camilla's eyes narrowed, but she didn't leap on the irony in his voice. "And we'll talk about this again."

That, Webb thought, *is precisely what I'm afraid of.*

*****

As the clock neared three, the mood of the students in the lecture hall shifted from attentive to restless. Papers shuffled, notebooks closed, books scraped as they were loaded into backpacks. Finally, in the middle of a sentence, the professor seemed to notice the time. "Test next Monday," he reminded, "after the Thanksgiving break." The rush to the door began.

Janey Griffin stayed in her seat at the back corner of the room, finishing up her notes and waiting for the traffic jam to clear. In a couple of minutes, she'd be able to walk straight through the building without having to dodge the crowds. Besides, she needed to finish writing down the professor's last line of logic before she left the room, because she'd never be able to reconstruct it tonight after work.

Outside the classroom, a petite blond was waiting for her, leaning against the wall with her books folded in her arms. She fell into step beside Janey. "Do you have time for a cup of coffee?"

Janey shook her head. "I'm due at work in an hour. You can walk over to the apartment with me if you like, and talk while I change clothes. What is it, Ellen? Boyfriend problems again?"

"Dennis is being a jerk." Ellen sounded almost absent-minded. "But that's nothing new. I can't believe you've still got this job."

"Why? I'm a good worker. In another month, I'll be finished with my probation, and I'll even get a raise—"

"And another noisy, greasy, disgusting machine to run."

"Somebody has to make drive shafts, honey, or your little red car would be a paperweight instead of transportation." Janey dodged traffic to cross the street which separated the campus from a residential area.

Ellen broke into a run to catch up. "But why does it have to be you? If you soak your hands for a year, you'll never get all the grease out of your skin. I can't believe you haven't quit by now."

"It's good money, and the hours are compatible with the classes I need to take. Besides, what would I do instead? Wait tables? Sorry, dear, but I'd rather smell of machine oil than french-fry grease. To say nothing of dealing with obnoxious customers..."

Which wouldn't be any easier than dealing with the jerks on the manufacturing line, she reminded herself.

Ellen seemed to have read her mind. "Are the men still harassing you?"

"Now and then," Janey admitted. She pulled out her keys as she ducked down the stairs beside a run-down old house to her apartment in the basement.

"What does that mean? Is it a constant hassle, or do they let you take breaks from it once in a while?" Ellen shook her head. "And you still haven't reported them?"

"What good would it do? I'd just get myself labeled as a troublemaker, which is hardly what I want before I'm even through my trial employment period. The things they do are never so clearly abusive that it's obvious, you know, or the supervisors would have seen it already."

"So go over their heads."

"Oh, right. I'll just march into Webb Copeland's office and announce that he has a bunch of sexist redneck jerks working on the manufacturing line. And I'm sure he'll promote me to corporate vice president and put me in charge of sensitivity training."

She pushed the door open. The apartment looked worse than usual, with her roommate's clothes and belongings strewn across the living room furniture.

Ellen looked around. "Has Kasey been hosting police raids? It looks like someone's been executing a search warrant in here."

Janey smiled. "Actually, it's an improvement over the upholstery. Kasey has better taste in clothes than the landlord does in furniture."

Ellen's face was tight. "You have a horrible job, you study the most incredible hours, you live in a rat hole..."

"Ellen, please—"

"I just hate it that you have to work so hard for this!" Tears gleamed in Ellen's eyes, and her fists clenched.

Janey said lightly, "Oh, it's good for my soul to work hard. Besides, it's what I get for not starting college on time. Since I had a job those few years in between and I actually made a little money, I can't get any real financial help now." She unearthed a box of tissues buried under a pile of Kasey's sweaters and handed it to Ellen.

Absently, Ellen pulled a tissue from the box. "Maybe my father could loan you some money."

"Don't you dare ask him," Janey ordered. "Even if he had the spare cash, it wouldn't be fair to put him on the spot. Anyway, I won't ask anybody to loan me money unless I can come up with something to offer as security—and that's about as likely as being struck by lightning. Look, Ellen, I know you only bring it up because you care. But being reminded of my circumstances doesn't change them, it just encourages me to feel sorry for myself."

Ellen sniffed and blew her nose. "I have never known you to feel sorry for yourself."

Janey smiled. "I'm glad to find out it doesn't show." She went into her tiny bedroom to change into the faded jeans and shabby flannel shirt she wore to work.

She wiped off her makeup, since in the factory's heat it would slide off her face anyway, and pulled her hair into a tight braid which would keep it out of reach of the machines she'd be running—and tried to put what Ellen had said out of her mind.

It wasn't as if anyone was holding a gun to her head, forcing her to live this way, Janey reminded herself. She'd chosen to sacrifice her living standard and to work at a job she didn't like because her long-term goals were more important.

In another couple of years, she'd be far enough along in her education to qualify for internships in her field, and she'd be able to build experience and develop contacts that would help in her eventual search for a full-time job. But most internships didn't pay, and even if she was lucky enough to land one of the few that did, she couldn't make enough money to support herself and finish her last year of school too.

So in the meantime she needed to put away all the money she could—and that meant for the next two years she'd be working the swing shift at Copeland Products.

Two more years of running noisy, messy machines, carving and bending solid metal into vehicle parts. Two more years of fellow employees who were unused to working side by side with women on the production line, men who vented their discomfort in crude remarks. Two more years of coming home after midnight exhausted and filthy, to be greeted by a stack of homework and an alarm clock already ticking ominously toward a too-early morning.

Two more years. It sounded like eternity.

Janey took a deep breath and forced herself to smile. She'd take it one day at a time, and she'd pull through... because she had to.

Teaser

1. What is Webb's problem at the start of the story?

2. What is Janey's problem at the start of the story?

3. How might the problems fit together? How might the characters cooperate?

4. How might the problems grow worse?

5. How might the problems eventually be solved?

Happy Endings

The most important thing about the ending of a book is that the issues between the characters are resolved in a way which is logical and satisfying to the reader. It's annoying to have two people who have hated each other all the way through the story fall into each others' arms on the last page and declare their devotion. It doesn't make sense. It's not logical, and it's not satisfying.

An equally unconvincing ending occurs when the core values of hero and heroine are so wildly different that it seems impossible for them ever to compromise. If he's a mink rancher and she's an animal-rights activist, it's a bit tough to believe that either of them can convince the other—and in a situation like that, there isn't a middle ground for compromise.

The happy ending is most believable when it requires both parties to make sacrifices for the sake of their love. This establishes a basic equality in the relationship, and it also makes it believable that they couldn't solve the problem earlier. A compromise also allows the author to add an element of surprise, in order to leave the reader thinking, "That's the perfect way for the story to end—why didn't I think of that?"

A resolved ending

A resolved ending means that any serious issues between hero and heroine are firmly settled, not just that one of them has made a vow to act differently.

A resolved ending means that if one of the characters makes a great sacrifice for the sake of the other, the reader is satisfied that the character will not later resent what he or she has given up.

A resolved ending answers all of the questions, including clearing up any reasons or motivations which have not been previously shared with the reader.

A resolved ending comes about because of the actions of the characters themselves, not through the interference of others.

The ultimate happy ending

The true test of a happy ending is how the reader feels as she turns the last page. Does she feel that this couple is truly committed to each other? Does she feel that they will be happy not just now but five years, ten years, fifty years from now?

Teaser

1. Think about the ending of a book you've recently read. What did you find satisfying about the way the story ended?

2. What did you find unsatisfying?

from
A Convenient Affair
(Harlequin Romance®, June 2001)

These two selections from *A Convenient Affair*, one from the beginning of the story and one from near the end, illustrate how elements from the start of a story can be used again in order to create a symmetrical ending. Watch for changes in the attitudes of the hero, Cooper Winston; the heroine, Hannah Lowe; and a pug named Brutus.

(From the first chapter)
Until that morning, Hannah had started to think it didn't matter what hour of the day or night she walked Mrs. Patterson's dog. If she abruptly decided to take Brutus out at two o'clock in the morning, she'd no doubt still run headlong into Cooper Winston somewhere along the way.

When she stopped to think about it, however, Hannah concluded that the wee hours of the night were actually one of the more likely times to encounter the occupant of the penthouse condominium. In the hours after midnight, he was apt to be just coming home to Barron's Court from a date... "And other associated activities," Hannah added under her breath.

Of course, she had also run into him at the crack of dawn, at high noon, and at nine-fifteen in the evening. The time seemed to be immaterial, the encounter inevitable.

Today, however, the chain appeared to have been broken. She and Brutus had gone all the way from Barron's Court up Grand Avenue to the governor's mansion and back, encountering their share of commuters and joggers and even a few bundled-up babies taking their mothers out for an airing in the autumn sunshine. But for once Hannah hadn't caught so much as a glimpse of a dark-haired, gray-eyed, broad-shouldered, supercilious six-foot hunk of testosterone named Cooper Winston.

By the time they once more reached the lobby of the condo complex, Brutus was breathing hard and Hannah could feel a glow throughout her whole body from the exercise and the crisp October breeze. She punched the button for the elevator and bent to release the pug's leash from his collar. "If you wouldn't pull so hard," she reminded him, "you wouldn't be out of breath at the end of your walk."

She hadn't heard the art deco doors open, but even before the man inside the elevator stepped into the lobby, she knew he was there. *So much for thinking my luck has changed,* she thought, and slowly straightened up, turning to face Cooper Winston.

She wasn't sure precisely why the hair at the back of her neck always stood straight up the moment he appeared on the scene. Probably sheer dislike, Hannah thought, coupled with a touch of apprehension—for there was no doubt that lately she was the one who had been coming out the worse for wear in their encounters. Whatever the reason, it was certainly a negative one; it wasn't as if there was anything she found magnetically attractive about the man.

Not that he was exactly hard on the eyes, she admitted. The first time she'd encountered him—over a negotiating table at Stephens & Webster, where she was an associate attorney—Hannah had thought Cooper Winston was extremely good-looking. She was partial to tall men with black hair and curly eyelashes and chiseled features. But of course that had been before she'd encountered the tight-set jaw, the perpetual crease between his brows, and the icy silver of his gaze.

All of which were in evidence right now.

She considered asking him—sweetly, of course—if he'd drunk his vinegar for breakfast as usual. But since there was nothing to be gained by gratuitous insults, she looked through him instead and said with cool politeness, "Good morning, Mr. Winston."

He didn't answer. She felt his gaze slide over her, and she was suddenly and painfully aware of her tousled hair, her wind-reddened cheeks, her far-from-new sweatsuit, and the faint aroma of dog that she'd acquired when she'd scooped up Brutus and carried him across Grand Avenue to beat a stream of traffic.

If the man dared to make a comment...

She looked straight at him, her chin held high.

Cooper didn't say a word. He didn't have to, Hannah thought bitterly. One dark eyebrow, lifting just a fraction of an inch, said it all.

At her feet, Brutus growled.

Cooper looked down. "You no doubt have some logical reason why this animal isn't on a leash, Ms. Lowe."

"Brutus has never bitten you," she pointed out.

"He's threatened often enough."

"Only because you make it so plain that you don't like him."

"What's to like? He's ugly, overweight, and ill-tempered."

"Being ugly isn't his fault," Hannah said crisply. "All pugs are. And if you were locked up all day, every day, in Mrs. Patterson's teeny little apartment, you'd probably be—" She bit her tongue, but it was already too late.

Cooper's voice was silky. "Overweight too? And even more ill-tempered than I already am?"

"I didn't say that."

"What a nice compliment you've paid Mrs. Patterson. She's quite a powerful woman, if merely being in her company could have such a destructive effect."

"Wait a minute! If you think I was saying that Mrs. Patterson is boring—" Hannah sputtered to a stop. He'd done it again, she admitted, irritated. Without even trying, he'd put her squarely in the wrong—and it wasn't much comfort to know that this time she'd handed him the opportunity.

"I'm sure you wouldn't dream of saying such a thing, Ms. Lowe. At least not where Mrs. Patterson might hear about it."

Hannah bristled. "I simply meant that her arthritis keeps her from taking Brutus for walks, so of course he's fat and irritable and not well-conditioned."

"But you've been exercising him for weeks now," Cooper pointed out, "and though he does seem to have slimmed down and stopped wheezing like a hippo, he's still in a bad mood all the time. What does that say about your company, Ms. Lowe?"

She smiled up at him. "Are you ever going to forgive me for interfering with your agreement to sell that restaurant chain, Mr. Winston? After all, I was only looking after my client's best interests. And the sale did eventually go through as you'd arranged, even though the terms were slightly altered."

"That's what you call *slightly altered?* Ms. Lowe, I'll forgive you about the same time I forget the fifteen million bucks your interference cost me."

Hannah feigned a sigh of relief. "Then, since fifteen million is pocket change to a man like you, I must be well on the way to rehabilitation."

"Fifteen million," he mused, "and all because you batted your eyelashes like an ingenue and asked a last-minute, breathless, innocent-sounding question."

"It wasn't like that."

"You mean it wasn't as innocent as it sounded? I'm glad you at least admit to being cold and calculating." He didn't give her an opportunity to answer, but strode across the lobby toward the street.

Just as well, Hannah thought. Brutus had only growled at him, as usual; Hannah herself would have been tempted to bite the man if he'd kept it up.

from
A Convenient Affair
(Harlequin Romance®, June 2001)

(From the last chapter)

Hannah and Brutus had gone all the way from Barron's Court up Grand Avenue to the governor's mansion and back, and by the time they reached the lobby again the pug was breathing hard.

The elevator was standing open. Hannah hurried the dog across the lobby, pushed the button for the fifth floor, and bent to release Brutus's leash from his collar. "How many times have I told you that if you didn't pull so hard you wouldn't be out of breath when—"

Just as the elevator doors began to close, the dog yipped and darted out into the lobby once more. Hannah, caught with his leash dangling, was stunned; Brutus had never done anything of the sort before. She jammed her hand between the doors, forced them open again, and went after him.

Brutus, yipping almost hysterically, made a bee-line for a man standing in the center of the lobby. From six feet away, he hurled himself at Cooper's knees; Cooper stooped to catch him and stood up with the pug in his arms.

Brutus snuffled at Cooper's shirt pocket, then sighed and settled down, his eyes half-closed and his neck stretched out so Cooper could more easily scratch his chin.

"That's disgusting," Hannah muttered. Of course, her conscience reminded, if she had been the one cuddled in Cooper's arms, she might look just as idiotically contented... "Thanks for capturing him. I'll take him off your hands now." She reached out for the dog.

Brutus opened his eyes halfway and growled at her.

Hannah's jaw dropped. "Listen, you stupid animal—"

"Brutus has never bitten you," Cooper pointed out. "And it's funny that you were never so concerned when he was growling at me on a regular basis."

"That was different." She caught herself. "I mean—"

"Never mind explaining. There are more important things to attend to just now. You agreed a few days ago that we were going to finish our talk—but then you ran away. And you've been very efficiently avoiding me ever since."

"I didn't run. I simply left, because I thought we'd said everything we needed to."

"Wrong—we still have a lot to say. As I see it, because you didn't stick around to discuss it then, you now have three choices. We either take up the discussion right here in the lobby, or you come upstairs with me where Daniel the doorman can't listen in."

"And my third choice?" Hannah asked warily.

He reached into his shirt pocket and held up a dog biscuit. Brutus perked up and barked, and Cooper gave him the treat. "I'll start carrying doggie candy in all my pockets, so anytime I'm within a block Brutus won't just run to me, he'll use his leash to drag you along." His fingers didn't stop their easy caress of the pug's chin. "What's so bad about talking to me, Hannah? Are you afraid I might knock a hole in that self-righteous armor of yours?"

She shrugged. "I don't have anything to say."

"Good. Then you can shut up and listen—because I do have a few things to tell you." With the dog still cradled in one arm, he took her elbow and guided her toward the elevator.

Teaser

1. What elements are the same in the two scenes?

2. What elements are different?

3. How has each character changed?

4. What events or actions might have caused these changes?

Reference

Romance Sub-Genres

(and how they can be distinguished from other kinds of women's fiction)

Within the general field of romance fiction, there are many distinctly different types. Books in each of the various types or sub-genres will have certain things in common, but the different lines, categories and types vary widely from each other.

Because the differences between romance and other forms of women's fiction are sometimes fuzzy, other types of books which are sometimes confused with romance are also listed here.

CATEGORY– Books which are published under a name brand, packaged with similar covers, and marketed as a group--which usually changes each month–rather than standing alone on the shelf. Books in each category will have certain things in common (for instance, they are all highly sensual or they all involve romantic intrigue). The books in each category will fall within fairly narrow limits on word count, though word counts vary widely between lines.

CHRISTIAN– See Inspirational.

CITY GIRL—Aimed at the reader in her twenties, this brand-new sub-genre has been inspired by the popularity of books like *Bridget Jones' Diary* and television shows such as *Sex in the City*. The heroine is younger and often less well established than more traditional romance heroines, and her conduct can be considerably less restrained. This is the one exception to the requirement for a permanent commitment, because City Girl books may end with the heroine finding "Mr. Right For Now" rather than "Mr. Right For All Time."

CONTEMPORARY– Occurring in the present day and dealing with realistic modern issues and problems, but generally avoiding mention of specific real people or current events which would tend to make the story seem outdated in a few years.

ETHNIC— Involving heroes and heroines of color (African-American or Hispanic are most common).

FUTURISTIC– An offshoot of paranormal involving romances taking place partially or entirely in the future. May involve time travel.

GAY– The exception to the rule that a romance novel is "the story of a man and a woman." Other than the sex of the partners, however, there are few differences between gay romance novels and straight romance novels. While they may have a few extra issues, partners in gay romances by and large experience the same sorts of conflicts as straight partners do, and they must make many of the same sorts of adjustments. A gay romance puts no more emphasis on the details of sexual encounters than a straight romance in an equivalent line would do.

HISTORICAL— Taking place in a past time. Most publishers of historicals prefer books set in Europe or North America and between 1066 (when William the Conqueror invaded England) and 1900. Longer than most romances, these stories can include some history and even social commentary, so long as it serves as background to the love story rather than sounding like a textbook. Though historical accuracy is important, heroines of historical romances tend to be modern—even feminist—in their attitudes. (Queen Elizabeth I went months at a time without brushing her teeth or taking a bath. The heroine of your historical probably shouldn't follow her example.)

INSPIRATIONAL– A romance in which the characters' religious faith, or their journey to develop faith in God, is a central part of the story. Though the religious background is usually non-denominational, most inspirationals are Christian and Protestant in orientation.

LINE— See Series.

LONG CONTEMPORARY— Longer books (over 70,000 words), allowing for more development of subplots and secondary characters, and frequently featuring sensuality as a strong element. These often include more latitude in types of characters (for instance, a hero with a mental illness) than the shorter books do, because there is more room to create reader empathy for the character.

MAINSTREAM— A single-title novel in which a romantic element may be present but is often not paramount. This is primarily the story of a heroine, and usually if the romance were to be removed, there would still be a story.

PARANORMAL— Including elements of science fiction or the supernatural, such as time travel, futuristic settings, witches, angels, vampires, genies, etc. Usually the setting and one (sometimes both) of the major characters are outside the normal limits of reality.

REGENCY— A branch of historical romance, set in Regency period England and involving the upper classes, often focusing on the main characters' efforts to make or escape the "right" marriage. Technically the Regency period ran from 1811 to 1820, but for literary purposes it is often stretched from the battle of Trafalgar in 1805 to the Reform Laws in 1834. Usually short (50,000 words) and sweet rather than sensual; the seamier side of life is seldom a large element. (A story in this time frame which involves darker elements is usually longer and is considered an historical set in the Regency period.)

ROMANTIC INTRIGUE— Including mystery, suspense, or threatening situations in which the heroine and/or hero are involved. Unlike a mystery or suspense novel which includes a love story, in a romantic intrigue, the romance is still the primary focus, though it often comes about because of the threat to the characters.

SAGA— A long novel which follows a female protagonist from early life to old age, usually including two generations of her descendants, though she remains the dominant character. Romance may be present but is not vital. Sagas are mainstream and single-title. They start out in an historical period but often end with the third generation in a contemporary time frame.

SERIES—(or LINE) The divisions within category romance. Each series or line will have elements in common and the books will be packaged with similar covers. (For example, Harlequin Romance is a sweet traditional story featuring emotional tension but little overt sexuality, and is about 50,000 words currently packaged in a cream-colored cover with a deep green stripe. Harlequin Temptation is a sensual story, usually with explicit sexuality, and is about 60,000 words, currently packaged in a dark red cover.) Each line has its own style and look in order to attract the reader's attention at the bookstore.

SHORT CONTEMPORARY— Generally considered the most sensual of the romance lines. Though these books usually include consummated sexual relationships between hero and heroine, their emphasis is still on love rather than sex. Usually 55,000 to 60,000 words.

SINGLE TITLE— Books which are free-standing, published and promoted without being part of a line or group of books. Single titles generally remain on the market and in print longer than category books. Single title books may be romance or mainstream.

SWEET TRADITIONAL— The original romance novel; a short

(50,000-55,000 words) book which is highly emotional and maintains sexual tension without including explicit love scenes. Some lines prefer that the hero and heroine not actually make love unless they're married (to each other, naturally) while others allow premarital sex. In either case, the emphasis of sensual description is on the feelings, not the act itself.

WOMAN IN JEOPARDY—The old-style Gothic romance is an example, but the rules have broadened considerably since Victoria Holt's day. The threat faced by the heroine in a woman-in-jeopardy book is bigger, fiercer, closer, and more frightening than in most romances (for instance, she might suspect her husband of trying to kill her). At present, this isn't as much a line or sub-genre in itself as it is a type of story which can be appropriate for several of the longer romance lines.

WOMEN'S FICTION— Encompasses single title and mainstream books. Written almost exclusively by women and predominantly for women, with a strong female protagonist but not necessarily a love story. Often involves a group of women who may be sisters, friends, or enemies.

YOUNG ADULT (YA)— Aimed at the teenage and even pre-teen reader, these books generally focus on the development of an innocent first love and include no sensual or sexual elements. A second YA line focuses on older teens and may involve realistic situations and decisions about drinking, drugs, premarital sex, etc. Though these books can carry a message, the successful ones don't preach or lecture.

Glossary

BODICE-RIPPER– Inspired by early historical romances which featured rape or rape fantasies, this derogatory term is still often applied to romance in general—usually by reporters or other people who don't read the books.

EROTICA– Stories which focus on the details of sexual encounters between the main characters or involving a main character and others. Though some erotica is romantic in nature, erotica and romance are not equivalent. Romance emphasizes the growing emotional connection between one couple, while erotica emphasizes sex and may include outside characters.

FORMULA– The famous "recipe" that is believed to exist which tells a writer exactly how to produce a saleable romance novel. In fact, the only formula for romance is the basic structure of a couple, a problem for them to solve, a once-in-a-lifetime love, and a happy ending.

GENRE– A distinctive type of literary composition. In current usage, genre refers to the various kinds of popular fiction (mystery, western, sci-fi, fantasy, romance), as opposed to literary fiction.

h/h– Shorthand for "hero and heroine." (for example, "I need my h/h to talk to each other but they won't cooperate.")

HOOK— The grabber which seizes the reader's attention and makes the book stand out from others. This often tells the reader what kind of book it is (marriage of convenience, secret baby) and is usually stated on the back cover.

MARRIAGE OF CONVENIENCE– A marriage entered into by the husband and wife for reasons other than love or physical attraction. Business, money, family, or child custody can all be reasons for a marriage of convenience.

OTHER WOMAN– Shorthand for any woman who is trying to interfere with or prevent the development of the hero's relationship with the heroine (other than family members). The other woman might be one the hero has dated, one who would like to date him, or an ex-wife or ex-fiancee.

SECONDARY CHARACTER– A character who is important but is not either the hero or the heroine. The story involves this character, but the story is not about this character.

SECRET BABY– A story about a couple whose past relationship resulted in a pregnancy, but the father was not told about the child.

SPICY– Preferred over "sexy" or "steamy" to describe the more sensual end of the romance spectrum.

SUB-GENRE–A further division or distinction between types within a genre. e.g, mystery can be divided into private investigators, citizen detectives, official police, etc.

TERTIARY CHARACTER– A character who fills a space and performs a function in the story but is not important enough to be fully developed. Tertiary characters often have only a single name (Ellen, John) or may not be named at all but referred to as "the butler" or "the manicurist."

VILLAIN– The bad guy. Not all romance novels have villains, and villains can range from being mildly unpleasant, trouble-causing individuals to being psychopaths or sociopaths.

Romance Publishers

The romance publishing industry changes on an almost daily basis. *Romance Writers' Report*, the professional journal of the Romance Writers of America, runs a monthly column which keeps members as up-to-date with the marketplace as possible. Attempting to do so in a book is impractical.

This is a list of commercial (royalty-paying) publishers who, at the time this book went to press, published romance novels and/or women's fiction. This list is not complete and is subject to change. An entry in this list does not imply endorsement or recommendation of the publisher.

This information is provided as a reference only and should not be relied on as a guide when submitting a manuscript. Romance lines, publishing schedules, market conditions, and editorial staff change quickly. Before submitting, check the current *Writer's Market* or the *Romance Writers' Report* (for RWA members) for correct street address and the name of the editor to whom submissions should be addressed.

Writer's Market also includes publishers' telephone numbers; it is appropriate to phone the company and ask for up-to-date information about how, where, and to whom your submission should be addressed.

The writer should familiarize himself or herself with the publisher's current books before submitting. This list makes no attempt to include the detailed information necessary for a writer to know which publishers would be most appropriate for the work.

Many publishers offer tip sheets or submission guidelines; a phone call to the editorial offices will tell you if the publisher you're interested in provides such information, which is usually sent free of charge to authors who provide a self-addressed envelope stamped with first class postage.

Hard copy- publishers:

Avalon Books– interested in hardcover romances, contemporary romances, and historical romances.

Avon Books– interested in historical and contemporary romance.

Ballantine/Ivy– interested in longer books with more complex plots and subplots. Guidelines available.

Bantam/Dell– interested in contemporary romances, historical romances.

Barbour Publishing/Heartsong Presents– interested in contemporary romances and historical romances.

Berkley/Jove– interested in historical romances, contemporary romances, paranormal romances, contemporary romantic suspense, and single-title mainstream. Guidelines available.

BET Books/Arabesque– interested in romance novels featuring heroes and heroines of non-Caucasian heritage (primarily African-American).

Dorchester Publishing– interested in historical romances, Gothic (woman in jeopardy) romances, contemporary romances, time-travel romances, futuristic romances and paranormal romances. Guidelines at www.dorchester.com or send SASE.

Genesis Press, Inc.– interested in African-American romance and erotica.

Harlequin Books–Canada– interested in sensual romances (Temptation), very sensual romances (Blaze), long contemporary romances (Superromance), romantic comedy (Duets).

Harlequin Mills & Boon–England–interested in contemporary romances (Harlequin Romance), medical romance, and historical romances.

Harlequin Books–New York– interested in romantic suspense (Intrigue) and contemporary romances (Harlequin American). Guidelines available.

HarperCollins/Avon– interested in young adult historical romances, contemporary romances, and historical romances.

ImiJinn Books– interested in paranormal romances, fairy tale romances, time-travel romances, romantic comedy, young adult books. Guidelines available at www.imajinnbooks.com.

Kensington Publishing– interested in contemporary romances, historical romances, Regency romances, multi-cultural romances, and women's mainstream fiction. Guidelines available at www.kensingtonbooks.com.

MIRA Books– interested in mainstream women's fiction including romantic suspense and family sagas.

Multnomah Publishers– interested in inspirational (Christian) romances. Guidelines at www.multnomahbooks.com.

New American Library– interested in Regency romance, contemporary romances, general women's fiction.

Pocket Books– interested in historical romances, general women's fiction.

Red Sage Publishing– interested in very sensual and spicy adult romance.

Silhouette Books– interested in sweet traditional romances, sensual romances, historical romances, long contemporary romances.

St. Martin's Press– interested in long contemporary romances, romantic suspense, historical romances, paranormal romance, and general women's fiction.

Steeple Hill– interested in inspirational contemporary romances. Guidelines available.

Tor/Forge– interested in general fiction, historical novels, paranormal, horror sf/fantasy and time travel, all of which may include romance as a factor– romance is not paramount.

Tyndale House– interested in historical and contemporary romances which are inspirational and Christian in nature. Guidelines available.

Warner Books– interested in single-title contemporary and historical romances, mainstream fiction.

Electronic publishers:

Books are available on the Internet for a fee; most publishers support downloads or can sell a book on diskette. Some also publish in trade paper.

Awe-Struck E-Books– www.awe-struck.net
DiskUs Publishing– www.diskuspublishing.com
Hard Shell Word Factory– www.hardshell.com

Leigh Michaels' Books

Harlequin Romance®

On September Hill   #2657   Nov 1984
Wednesday's Child   #2734   Dec 1985 (Reprinted 1999)
Come Next Summer   #2748   Feb 1986
Capture A Shadow   #2806   Dec 1986
O'Hara's Legacy   #2830   Apr 1987
Sell Me A Dream   #2879   Dec 1987
Strictly Business   #2951   Dec 1988
Just A Normal Marriage   #2987   Jun 1989
Shades of Yesterday   #2997   Aug 1989
No Place Like Home   #3010   Oct 1989
Let Me Count The Ways   #3023   Dec 1989
A Matter of Principal   #3070   Aug 1990
An Imperfect Love   #3086   Nov 1990
An Uncommon Affair   #3119   Apr 1991
Promise Me Tomorrow   #3141   Aug 1991
Temporary Measures   #3160   Nov 1991
Garrett's Back In Town   #3171   Jan 1992
Old School Ties   #3184   Mar 1992
The Best-Made Plans   #3214   Aug 1992
The Unexpected Landlord   #3233   Nov 1992
Safe In My Heart   #3248   Feb 1993
Ties That Blind   #3263   May 1993
The Lake Effect   #3275   Aug 1993
Dating Games   #3290   Nov 1993
A Singular Honeymoon   #3300   Feb 1994
Traveling Man   #3311   May 1994
Family Secrets   #3326   Aug 1994   (Reprinted 2001)
The Only Solution   #3337   Nov 1994
House of Dreams   #3343   Jan 1995
Invitation To Love   #3352   Mar 1995
Taming A Tycoon   #3367   Jul 1995
The Unlikely Santa   #3388   Dec 1995
The Only Man For Maggie   #3401   Mar 1996
The Daddy Trap   #3411   Jun 1996
Marrying the Boss!   #3423   Sep 1996
The Perfect Divorce   #3444   Feb 1997
Baby You're Mine!   #3463   Jul 1997
The Fake Fiancé   #3478   Oct 1997

The Billionaire Date   #3496   Mar 1998
The Playboy Assignment   #3500   Apr 1998
The Husband Project   #3504   May 1998
Her Husband-To-Be   #3541   Feb 1999
The Boss and the Baby #3552 May 1999 (Reprinted 2001)
The Tycoon's Baby   #3574   Oct 1999
Husband on Demand   #3600   Apr 2000
Bride on Loan   #3604   May 2000
Wife on Approval   #3608   Jun 2000
The Corporate Wife   # 3628 Nov 2000
The Bridal Swap   # 3637 Jan 2001
A Convenient Affair   # 3656 Jun 2001
His Trophy Wife   #3672 Sep 2001
Backwards Honeymoon   #3691   Mar 2002
The Boss's Daughter   #3711   Aug 2002
Bride by Design   #3720   Nov 2002
Maybe Married   early 2003
The Marriage Market   mid 2003

Harlequin Presents®
Kiss Yesterday Goodbye #702   Jun 1984 (Reprinted 1994)
Deadline For Love   #811   Aug 1985
Dreams to Keep   #835   Nov 1985
Touch Not My Heart   #876   Apr 1986
Leaving Home   #900   Jul 1986
The Grand Hotel   #1004   Aug 1987
Brittany's Castle   #1028   Nov 1987
Carlisle Pride   #1049   Feb 1988
Rebel With A Cause   #1068   Apr 1988
Close Collaboration   #1107   Sep 1988
A New Desire   #1147   Feb 1989
Exclusively Yours   #1162 Apr 1989 (Reprinted 2000)
Once and For Always   #1245   Feb 1990
With No Reservations   #1266 May 1990

Category romances such as Harlequin Romances® and Harlequin Presents® are sometimes hard to find even just a few weeks after publication. Bookstores can special-order recent titles from their distributors. On-line sources for current and recent titles include www.bn.com . Older titles can sometimes be located at www.alibris.com – a nation-wide alliance of bookstores who have posted their inventories in a searchable database online.

Suggested Reading

Bickham, Jack M. **Scene and Structure: How to construct fiction with scene-by-scene flow, logic and readability**. (Writer's Digest Books: 1993). ISBN 0-89879-551-6. An excellent aid to creating logical and believable plots.

Browne, Renni & Dave King. **Self-Editing for Fiction Writers.** (HarperCollins: 1993) ISBN 0-06-272046-5. A concise manual using published examples and exercises to improve the writer's command of basics.

Dixon, jay (sic). **The Romance Fiction of Mills & Boon.** (UCL Press: 1999.) ISBN 1-85728-267-1. A history and analysis of romance fiction as published by the first large-scale romance publisher.

Johnson, Victoria M. **All I Need to Know in Life I Learned From Romance Novels.** (General Publishing Group: 1998.) ISBN 1-57544-101-2. In this light-hearted look at how the romance novel applies to real life, the author also details the special features and rules of romances.

Krentz, Jayne Ann. **Dangerous Men and Adventurous Women.** (University of Pennsylvania Press, 1992.) ISBN 0-8122-1411-0. Essays by various romance writers on why the romance novel is so popular.

Romance Writer's Report. Professional journal of the Romance Writers of America, published monthly. Available only to members. Visit www.rwanational.org for more information.

Writer's Market. (Writer's Digest Books: annual.) Market listing of publications, including book publishers, magazines, and others.

Index

Do you have questions about submitting your manuscript? About query letters, sample chapters, and synopses? About multiple submission and how long to wait for an answer? About agents and copyrights? About commercial publishing, subsidy publishers, and self-publication? About rejection letters? About pen names, revisions, contracts and royalties?

The book you need is

Dear Leigh Michaels...
A Novelist Answers the Most-Asked Questions about Getting Published

As a bonus with your purchase of *Creating Romantic Characters*, the publisher of both books will send you *Dear Leigh Michaels* –a $9.95 value–for only the cost of postage and handling.

Please send check or money order for $3.95 (in Canada, please send $4.95 in US funds), along with the proof of purchase below, to

> Dear Leigh Michaels
> PBL Limited
> P.O. Box 935
> Ottumwa IA 52501-0935.

Act Now– Limited Time Offer
Supplies cannot be guaranteed
Offer available in the United States and Canada only.
If your order cannot be filled, your check will be returned.

Creating Romantic Characters
PROOF OF PURCHASE
clip this corner and mail